B890

CULTURE

Prepared for the course team by Derek Pugh
with contributions by Allan Plath

International Enterprise

The Open University
BUSINESS SCHOOL

OPEN UNIVERSITY COURSE TEAM

Core group

Dr Allan Plath, *Course Team Chair*
Mr Jon Billsberry, *Critical Reader*
Mr Martin Brazier, *Graphic Designer*
Mr Eric Cassells, *Author*
Dr Timothy Clark, *Author*
Ms Karen Dolan, *Course Manager*
Mrs Shirley Eley, *Course Team Assistant*
Ms Ann Faulkner, *Liaison Librarian*
Ms Julie Fletcher, *Editor*
Mr Mike Green, *Critical Reader*
Mrs Cherry Harris, *Course Team Assistant*
Dr Nick Heap, *Author*
Mr Roy Lawrance, *Graphic Artist*
Dr Richard Mole, *Production Director, OUBS*
Prof. Derek Pugh, *Author*
Prof. Janette Rutterford, *Author*
Ms Linda Smith, *Project Controller*
Prof. Andrew Thomson, *Author*
Mr Steve Wilkinson, *BBC Series Producer*

External consultants

Dr Jim Attridge, *Critical Reader*
Dr David Barnes, *Author*

Prof. Peter Dicken, *Author*
Prof. John Drew, *Author and Editor of the Reader*
Prof. Nigel Grimwade, *Author*
Prof. Malcolm Hill, *Author*
Prof. Paul Iles, *Author*
Mr Ian McCall, *Author*
Dr David Silk, *Author*
Dr Steve Tallman, *Author*
Prof. Monir Tayeb, *Author*

Developmental testers

Ms Barbara Awuku-Asabre
Mr Ian Cooley
Dr Alan Eggleston
Mr David Milton
Mr Roy Needham
Mr Fred Thomson

External assessors

Prof. Dr Pervez N. Ghauri, *University of Groningen, The Netherlands*
Prof. Simon Coke, *Edinburgh University Management School, Edinburgh*

The Open University, Walton Hall, Milton Keynes MK7 6AA

First published 1995, second edition 1999. Reprinted 1999, 2001

Edited, designed and typeset by The Open University.

Printed in the United Kingdom by Selwood Printing Ltd., Burgess Hill, West Sussex

ISBN 0 7492 7687 8

For further information on Open University Business School courses and the Certificate, Diploma and MBA programmes, please contact the Course Sales Development Centre, The Open University, PO Box 222, Walton Hall, Milton Keynes MK7 6YY (tel: 01908 653449).

oubs.open.ac.uk

2.3

19040B/b890cui2.3

CONTENTS

INTRODUCTION

'There are no foreign lands; only the traveller is foreign.'

Robert Louis Stevenson

'Nothing will be done any more without the whole world meddling in it.'

Paul Valéry

BACKGROUND TO THE UNIT

It is common sense that things are done differently in different cultures. Ask any manager with experience outside their home culture, and you will find a favourite 'war story' about the difficulties or peculiarities of the ways things get done in country X or region Y. Whole books point out, with tongue in cheek, the blunders made by managers who have not fully appreciated just how profound these differences are.

Clearly, there are international differences but the key issue is: how important are they? Managers of international enterprises need to know whether the workings of organizations in one country are completely different from those in another. They also need to understand how knowledge of their home country organization and its functioning would help them in dealing with other places in the world. A key question for managers of international enterprises is: are the structures and functions of organizations in different cultures sufficiently close together so that universally applicable approaches can be developed with the expectation of obtaining consistent outcomes?

Do, for example, the differences in organizational functioning between the UK and France and Germany matter? Is managing an organization in the developing world fundamentally different and likely to remain so? Or are organizations all over the world converging so that differences in management are becoming less and less important, and increasingly merely quaint? This unit examines these differences. It then considers how far along this convergent path organizations have already travelled and how far the influence of specific cultural factors must be understood and planned for if a manager is to be effective in international enterprise.

AIMS AND OBJECTIVES

The unit's main aims are to:

- Recognize the impact of differences in national cultures on the activity of managing in an international setting.
- Highlight those differences in national cultures which have been shown to have an impact on management functioning in international situations, often with unfortunate results.
- Demonstrate that some managerial activities are converging world wide.
- Increase sensitivity to cultural differences and thus help to improve interpersonal effectiveness in cross-cultural situations.

- Analyse the process of 'culture shock' and explore how it can be understood and managed – although never avoided.

When you have completed this unit, you should be able to:

- Be aware of the impact of your management activities on cultures other than your own.
- Be more culturally sensitive in interpersonal relationships in cross-cultural situations.
- Analyse which aspects of international operation are subject to convergence across cultures.
- Understand the phenomenon of culture shock, in order to manage your way through it better.

OVERVIEW OF THE UNIT

This unit has five sections. In Section 1 we state the problem of the impact of cultural differences on the operation of international management, recognizing that, while it is considerable, it is not unlimited. In Section 2 we review the evidence for a convergence of global management functioning, and in Section 3 attempt to make sense of systematic cultural differences in management around the world. In Section 4 we ask: what makes an effective cross-cultural manager? We start by considering the phenomenon of culture shock and how effective managers find their way through it. Then we look at the characteristic styles of more effective international managers, and examine the types of training which have been found to be helpful in developing effectiveness in cross-cultural situations. Section 5 discusses cultural change and helps to point the way to better, more sensitive, cultural functioning.

Note. In Section 1.3 there is a brief discussion of stereotypes, which points out that, despite the negative overtones of the term, stereotyping is useful if viewed with caution. Throughout this unit we consciously employ stereotypes as a way of making a point. Remember that these oversimplifications are used deliberately for teaching purposes. Note also the important distinction made in Table 4 in Section 4.2 about the use of public and private stereotypes by international managers.

1 THE EFFECTS OF CULTURE

1.1 COPING WITH NEW MARKETS

On a cold night in Warsaw in the winter of 1992, half a million people received a free introductory sachet of *Pert-Plus* hair shampoo through their letter boxes. The manufacturers, Procter & Gamble, had decided to use one of their standard marketing exercises to heighten awareness of their product and to tempt new customers to try it. That night two thousand letter boxes were rifled, and the next morning stolen sachets were on sale at every street corner. The company had to pay for numerous letter boxes to be repaired.

But the story has a happy outcome! As a result of the publicity generated by the thefts, the product reached its targeted annual sales level for Poland after only one month.

Unfortunately, not all stories of attempts to cope with new markets by assuming that they are like old ones have a happy ending as in the example above (reported in the *Guardian*, 7 June 1993). When General Motors (that is, Vauxhall and Opel) proudly introduced their new Nova model in South America, they were disappointed at its poor sales until it was pointed out to them that '*no va*' in Spanish and Portuguese means 'it doesn't go'! Bertlesmann, the vast German-based multinational publisher, does a lot of subscription book club publishing in English. It considered the market in India to be most attractive since millions of educated Indians read and speak English. But a book club relies on the operation of a viable postal address system, and most Indians have unreliable addresses. After several expensive test campaigns concentrating on urban areas, Bertelsmann realized that from a population of almost a billion it had a potential market of only about 200,000 actual subscribers, with little room for growth. The company had to pull out of India after considerable losses.

Examples of managers' inadequate understanding of different countries' ways can be multiplied almost indefinitely. To be effective in different cultural situations, there is no alternative to doing a great deal of homework in order to understand what factors are distinctive. Volvo, for example, has applied the concept of variable advertising in different cultures very effectively. It has emphasized economy in the USA, durability in the UK, status in France, performance in Germany, safety in Switzerland, price in Mexico, and quality in Venezuela.

So there are important differences which enterprises, and the managers within them, have to recognize and cope with in international operations. But not everything will be different. There will also be important similarities across countries. In the Volvo example, it is the marketing that changes. The products are basically the same, with clear limited variations (left-hand drive, seat belts, to conform to the national regulations; engine adjustments for climate differences, for example in humidity). Compare this with the fact that in the 1980s there were more than 500 national versions of the Peugeot 505, which led to increased production costs, excess documentation, country specific spare parts, etc. – all disadvantages to profitability.

By contrast, IKEA, the Swedish-based home furnishings retailer, has become the largest global operator in its sector in the world through a standardized product strategy which offers the identical product range world wide. On the other hand, Coca-Cola alters elements in its marketing mix such as price positioning and product composition (being sweeter in the Middle East), but always maintains the high visibility of its global brand logo. So an important skill is to be able to recognize which aspects of organization functioning can be replicated across countries and which must be changed to be effective in a particular national culture.

By the term 'culture' we refer to the distinctive way of life of a nation or ethnic grouping. Culture is shown in the way that tasks are carried out, social institutions function and members of the nation or grouping think and communicate. Once the distinctive values and appropriate behaviours of a culture have been learnt by members in early life they tend to persist unconsciously. They normally do not have to be discussed since they are taken for granted. They come to the fore only when we go into another culture and discover, often with unpleasant surprise, that people think about things and do them differently there.

No culture is static. All cultures are continually gradually changing as the situation changes. Although the particular combination of characteristics will be distinctive for each culture, there are also considerable similarities across cultures in many respects. In this unit we shall focus on the causes of similarities and differences in management operations in different countries. In particular, we shall need to get some understanding of other cultures if we are to manage well in them.

1.2 WORLD-WIDE FACTORS AFFECTING MANAGEMENT

We need to become skilled at operating in countries other than our own. Is this skill all a matter of understanding a country's culture? If firms in Ghana do not plan, budget and market their products in ways that are taught in the Open University Business School MBA programme, is this because their traditional culture hinders effective management? Well, maybe. But remember they may be supplying local markets which take all their products, so the cost of using sophisticated techniques would be unjustified. Is the speed of investment decisions in Brazil due to a culture which values fast action, or to hyperinflation which removes financial gains unless they are reaped quickly? Is the centralization of management decisions in Egyptian firms due to a culture where people wait for a lead from the top, or to the fact that most are state-owned enterprises, a condition which leads to centralization everywhere?

It is not easy to disentangle completely or with any precision what is due to a country's culture. After all, we can always argue that everything that happens is interlinked. The small scale of operation in Ghana, hyperinflation in Brazil, and government ownership in Egypt may themselves be the outcome of the cultures that foster them. But it helps to see the world as multi-causal, and not to regard culture as a catch-all concept used to 'explain' everything, because that approach would become too diffuse and explain nothing. In order to be able to use the concept of culture effectively in explanation, we need to be aware of a number of important other factors which will influence the operations of an international enterprise.

Some influences on the way enterprises function clearly apply across all cultures.

1 The size of the unit of operation. Larger organizations will require more impersonal forms of management than smaller ones.

2 The level of technological development in operation. High capital investment will produce technologies that require more technically sophisticated ways of operating and better trained workforces.

3 The institutional environment of the enterprise. Joint stock companies will require different styles of operation from government enterprises which, in turn, will differ from family-owned businesses.

4 The different managerial roles. The functional jobs that managers do (for example, production, marketing), their level in the hierarchy (for example, chief executive, first line supervisor), the training and education they have received (for example, engineer, linguist) will all produce characteristic differences in outlook.

5 The 'organizational culture'. Organizations develop their own cultures (another term to help distinguish this from national culture is organizational ethos) and in international enterprises this will have some impact across subsidiaries in all national cultures (for example, ICI, McDonalds, Mitsubishi, Nestlé).

6 The physical attributes of the product. These will put demands on the manufacturing firm wherever it is located. In Section 2.1 we explore in more detail the necessary organizational and social requirements for companies who manufacture motor cars anywhere in the world. Similarly the requirements for the efficient manufacture of telephone equipment or personal computers will have much in common all over the world. This will encourage globalization of production on grounds of cost, and this in turn will lead to the globalization of the market demand for product performance. For example a French government-backed attempt in the 1980s to offer a 'simplified' computer for developing countries was a complete failure, being resented and rejected by the potential markets.

The above influences will be apparent across all cultures. This means that there will be important similarities as well as differences in the way organizations operate in different countries, as the examples above illustrate. In Section 2, we shall consider the argument that these factors, and others like them which we have not listed, are getting stronger. As enterprises move more and more to operate internationally they are producing a convergence in management functioning which, in due course, will mean that there will be a common global management 'culture'. Thus we are heading for the management analogue of the 'global village', where thinking is always in terms of global production, global markets and global communications. For example, as a result of the global recession of the early 1990s, the Volkswagen Motor Company in Germany, faced with the unprecedented need of having to make redundancies in the workforce, invented the 'four day week'. This was an innovative deal with the Works Council which reduced the working week to 28 hours, with a reduction in wages but a guarantee of no redundancies (Scholz, 1996). If VW show this system to be efficient and profitable, how long will it be before automobile workers in other countries faced with redundancies will press for and obtain the same conditions? Hence the quotation from Paul Valéry at the beginning of this unit.

Activity 1

Assume you are visiting a firm in Japan, but do not read Japanese. At the reception desk your contact hands you the diagram below. Would you have any clue as to what it represented before it was explained and translated for you?

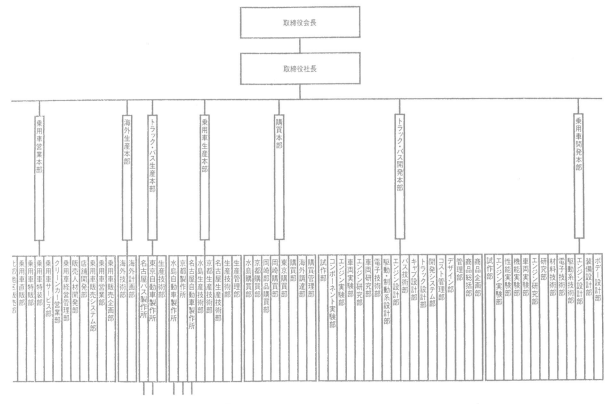

Figure 1   (Source: Hickson and Pugh, 1995)

Comment

As an experienced manager, you will probably have spotted it as an organization chart even before your contact started to speak. In fact, it is an extract from the organization chart of the Mitsubishi Motors Corporation. But most large organizations in most countries in the world could produce a chart on similar lines, thus demonstrating the world-wide impact of the size of the unit of operation.

1.3 KEY MANAGEMENT-RELATED ELEMENTS OF CULTURES

Global convergence will be some way off, if it happens at all. We must also be aware that other countries are different in important ways that affect management. The quotation from Robert Louis Stevenson at the beginning of this unit underlines the need for international managers to approach other cultures with respect. In particular, it is important to avoid automatically judging them in terms of our own culture – and inevitably finding them wanting.

There are some elements of culture that recur frequently enough in cross-cultural problems to suggest that they are of key importance in relation to managing. It is important for an international manager to get a feel for these aspects of any new culture – and it is vital to be able to recognize the differences in a non-judgemental way and not immediately condemn them.

Attitudes to authority

The authority of superiors in all organizations in all societies rests on a mix of position or status and personal competence. But the mix varies. In some countries competence matters more than status and leads to promotion. However, even in the most competence-oriented cultures, sons and daughters of a firm's founder, for example, are likely to wield greater authority than colleagues with no family connections. In cultures where position, status, caste and family matter much more than in the West in exercising authority, Westerners might jump to the conclusion that this must be inefficient. This is not necessarily so. If, to command respect in order to exercise authority effectively, a manager needs wider social standing, connections and so on, then to pass over such a person for promotion just because a more technically competent person without these attributes is available would not be sensible, since it would be perceived as an affront. It would be felt as such by subordinates too, and would disturb the workings of the organization. The key point to remember is that, whatever the relative weightings given to competence or position, every cultural system is taken by its own members to be 'natural, right and proper'.

Even within Europe there are considerable variations in attitudes to authority. The example below from Hickson and Pugh (1995) illustrates a major difference between Spain, where hierarchy is emphasized, and Sweden, one of the most egalitarian countries in the world.

> The British general manager (Europe) of an American-owned world-wide multinational corporation based in Paris, described the practical difficulties of working across cultures in an international network:
>
> 'In Spain it is comparatively easy to know who to deal with. When I visit our Spanish subsidiary company and walk through the door into a meeting of executives, I can tell instantly who is the chairman – even if I have not met him [sic] before. He has a more imposing bearing, everyone is sitting slightly angled towards him with a respectful demeanour, and all conversation is directed to and from him.
>
> 'But in Stockholm, if I do not know the Swedish chief executive by sight, I can be in trouble. They are all sitting around at ease, in casual shirts, talking generally. I can't readily tell who the CE is. It can be embarrassing.'

Attitudes to others

In all societies, children are born into families. But there are wide variations in how 'the family' is defined. In the West the family is limited to the 'nuclear' family – parents and their children, with possibly a grandparent living in. In other societies, the 'extended' family formed by the wide network of brothers, cousins, uncles, aunts, grandparents, great-aunts and so on is the group with which a person identifies. And it can go wider still, with clans or castes being the important social group. The importance for organizations is that the identification that the individual has been taught to accept will have considerable impact on relationships at work. Where there is a strong emphasis on the extended family, family loyalties are very strong and people will look to fulfil family obligations in work by, for example, obtaining jobs for their relations. So 'nepotism', far from being a sin or even a crime, is a virtue, strongly upheld. In a nuclear family culture, 'businesslike' (impersonal) relationships are appropriate at work. People may be embarrassed if relatives came to work in the same place. The example below (reported in Adler, 1991) shows the misunderstandings that these differences can cause, and underlines how members of both cultures think that their way is natural, right and proper.

A JOB FOR MY DAUGHTER

Rad, an engineer who had emigrated to Germany from the former Yugoslavia, worked for a German engineering firm. His daughter Lana had recently graduated from a German university. Rad considered it his duty to find his daughter a job and he wanted his German boss, who had a vacancy, to hire Lana. Although the boss felt that Lana was extremely well qualified for the position, he refused to have a father and daughter working in the same office. The very suggestion of hiring family members was repugnant to him. Rad believed his boss was acting unfairly – he could see no problem in his daughter working with him in the same office.

The outcome was that Lana was not taken on for the job, nor even considered. The boss lost respect for Rad, and Rad became so upset that he asked for a transfer to a different department. Neither of them understood that the conflict was caused by different cultural approaches to appropriate relationships with others.

Attitudes to managing yourself

How you see yourself in relation to what you wish to achieve is an important factor affected by the culture in which you were brought up. Is it more important for you to gain achievement, or to develop yourself in ways that express personal qualities, good experiences, social harmony? Is achieving the goal more important than the processes involved? Is the emphasis on doing or being? Again, in our achievement-oriented Western world, it is sometimes difficult to believe that others take a different view. But they do. For example, many Westerners in Malaysia have discovered that giving a wage increase to those who value 'being' has ensured that they reduce the hours worked.

Even in the West there is the classic distinction between German and British managers in attitudes to the place of humour in management. A study by Ebster-Grosz and Pugh (1996) found that both British and German managers agree that Britons are more relaxed and regard humour as acceptable in any management situation – 'It helps to make the wheels go round'. German managers, on the other hand, believe that business is a serious matter and joking about it is inappropriate. And not only managers think this, as Toyota (Germany) discovered. The firm put out a humorous advertisement for its cars showing singers dressed as apes. The advertisement got a very high recognition and approval rating, but Toyota's market share fell by more than 12 per cent. The German view is that someone who spends that amount of money on a car doesn't want to buy a joke. But British advertisements often feature humour (reported in the *Guardian*, 20 June 1998).

Attitudes to time

Some cultures have a 'monochronic' notion of time. The clock is steadily ticking away; the 'unforgiving minute' should be filled with 'sixty seconds' worth of distance run', and 'time is money'. Others have what Hall (1976) calls a 'polychronic' perception. In this case, time is an endless rolling cycle; it is multi-track and many things can be done at once. Queues can wait patiently in the offices of officials in, say, India and then be told to come back tomorrow. Time can be taken to get to know business visitors and create trust. Arriving at the stated time matters less in Latin America than properly finishing the social proprieties of the previous business engagement. A British manager in Argentina who is kept waiting for over half an hour after the appointment is due may well feel that this is something to do with establishing relative status, or even a negotiating ploy. But it is not, and in turn the British manager will get all the time that is necessary for the discussion – to the consternation of the next monochronic caller! The striking European example below was described by Hall (1976).

> ## POLYCHRONIC TIME
>
> A German manager who arrives in Paris to negotiate a contract with a French supplier will probably have to give up any preconceived notions of setting to work immediately and concluding in time to return to Frankfurt that night. The manager will be appalled at finding that the French contact will spend much of the morning deciding, after lengthy consultation with everyone present, where to eat lunch.
>
> The German does not speak the French language of time, which requires evoking the whole gustatory apparatus and setting the proper interpersonal relationship before business can be taken up. If the German insists on adhering to a rigid schedule, the French supplier will label the visitor as uncouth, someone with little appreciation of life and no feeling for people.

It is important to understand that there is nothing frivolous or trivial about such situations. The principles of behaviour for people, like the French, who work on a polychronic system of time are just as binding as those in cultures, like the German, which work on a monochronic system. Managers from a monochronic system should allocate at least three days on initial contact to allow their French colleagues to adjust to their physical presence in Paris or Lyons. This allows the French to rearrange life accordingly, and the visitors can use the first few days for activities that are not specifically related to business. This will be time well spent. It allows the visitors to make their presence known and to become acquainted with their hosts. Talking informally about matters other than business during the first few days will content everyone and will pay off later. It is essential to observe these rules for behaviour in France because a characteristic of polychronic cultures is a deep involvement with people. Monochronic cultures are much more concerned with procedures and agendas.

Attitudes toward nature

Trompenaars (1993) points out that the ways in which cultures relate to the natural world vary considerably. For example, certain tribes of Native Americans consider themselves to be part of the fabric of a living whole world. They are not masters of this world, they are not subjects to it, they are it. All that they are, all that they do, is part of the great whole that surrounds them, and this leads to a respect for the existence of everything – rocks, trees, insects, sheep and other people.

Compare this to the technological cultures of the West. 'The world is our oyster.' We humans command it, we control it. There is a strict hierarchy of existence in our philosophy. Rocks are seen as less valuable than 'living things', animals are worth more than plants, and humans are worth more than other animals.

Trompenaars asked people from different cultures to choose between the following two statements:

A   It is worth while trying to control important natural forces, like the weather.
B   Nature should take its course and we just have to accept it the way it comes and do the best we can.

His results reveal some interesting differences between countries, as shown in Figure 2.

Only two countries (Brazil and Portugal) had a majority of individuals choosing statement A. It would be a worthwhile (and not totally inaccurate) generalization to say that these countries' cultures are likely to have a stronger sense that nature is perfectible and controllable. Three countries (Egypt, Japan and Czechoslovakia) had around 10 per cent of the people surveyed agreeing with the statement. Again, we could generalize and suggest that these countries' cultures see less purpose in controlling nature. The point here is the tremendous variation in the ways in which various cultures relate to nature.

The relationship between humans and nature has long been a major difference between cultures. We need only think of the ways in which the Americans and the British regard their pets. Compare this with the way that animals are dealt with in Spain.

Variability within cultures

Figure 2 suggests another point for you to notice: in no culture will there be universal agreement about the ideas that underlie the culture. That is to say that, in any given country, there will be people who hold cultural values quite strongly and those who hold them not at all. It is as easy to imagine individuals (to use the example above) in the UK who do not value attempts at intervention, and those in Argentina who do.

The attribution of cultural traits to individuals from a given culture is called 'stereotyping'. The word has negative connotations, but you should be aware that stereotyping is not necessarily bad. In fact, it is a natural outgrowth of the ways in which we communicate.

See Nancy Adler's comments on stereotyping in video 3.

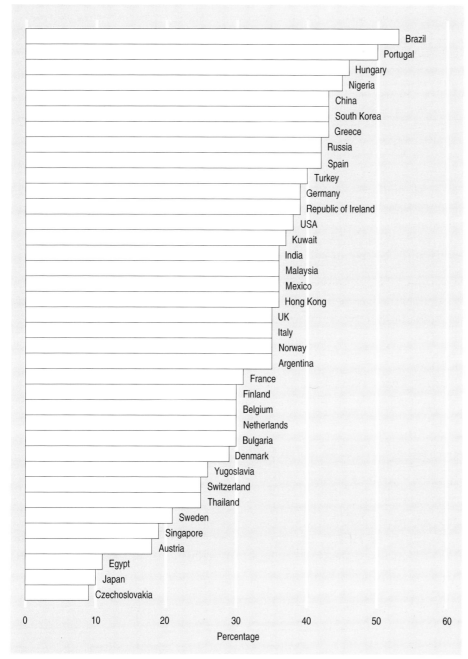

Figure 2   Percentage of respondents in different countries who chose statement A
(adapted from Trompenaars, 1993, p. 127)

It is important to note the following about stereotypes.

- Stereotypes are automatic, and cannot be avoided. They are the ways in which we organize our thinking in new situations.

- Stereotypes are derived either from experience with members of other groups or from secondary sources. In either case, they arise because we have too little accurate information to go on.

- Stereotypes can be moved closer to reality by increased contact with the group that is being stereotyped.

- If the stereotyper's perception of another group is positive or neutral the stereotype will be (wrongly) that the other group is 'just like us'.

- Stereotypes, in and of themselves, do not lead to miscommunication. The problems arise if they are inaccurate and are held too rigidly. Then, the predictions made by them will be wrong, and this will lead to misunderstanding.

- If we want to communicate effectively with strangers, we should not seek to avoid stereotypes. What we need to do is to increase the complexity and accuracy of our stereotypes. We do this by constantly questioning them.

1.4 CONCLUSION

This section has suggested that, on the surface, culture seems problematic. If we look deeper into the topic though, we see that the aspects of cultures that are relevant to managers have much in common. This comes about because forces of size, technology and the like press organizations towards convergence in the ways they operate. On the other hand, cultures do have unique elements within them that must be understood. These cultural features arise from our attitudes towards authority, others, self and nature.

The characteristic cultural differences that have an influence on management will be examined further in Section 3. There we shall be discussing a systematic way of classifying cultures in relation to work values which offers a set of 'cultural maps' of the world. Even if we accept that each cultural configuration is to a considerable degree distinct, the classification should enable a manager from one culture to get some degree of prior understanding of another one.

- authority
- other
- self
- nature

2 CONVERGENCE IN GLOBAL MANAGEMENT FUNCTIONING?

We have highlighted some of the issues with which this unit is concerned. In this section we shall review the evidence for global convergence in managerial functioning.

The argument is that we are seeing a world-wide development of industrialization, technology, large scale of operation, and interdependence of multi-organizational systems. All of these require an instrumentally rational approach to achieve the levels of performance required for an organization to survive. Cultural differences are therefore becoming of less and less importance. What matters in understanding the management in a particular country are world-wide factors such as its level of economic development, foreign investment and technological sophistication. The scale of industrial operations in a country, and its access to global communications, are among the key factors.

2.1 THE PROCESS OF INDUSTRIALIZATION

The convergence debate was inaugurated in the 1960s by Kerr and his colleagues at Harvard University (Kerr *et al.*, 1960). They argued that industrialism is world wide. It is based on science and technology, which speak in a universal language. Science is supranational, independent of the form of government or the culture of a people. Technology spreads out so that the world is apparently divided into countries that are industrialized and those that are in the process of becoming so. In Kerr's view, this is the major transition and all countries will participate in the inevitable industrialization.

The spread of industrial technology from the more developed nations occurs in four main ways:

1   through the normal channels of trade when developing countries buy products and manufacturing facilities

2   through imitation, for example, when they set up technical schools and colleges or distance-learning universities

3   through the effects of economic aid, which usually involves the delivery of more advanced technology and workforce training

4   through military channels, since the world-wide scope of military confrontation has led to the training of workforces to build bases, maintain vehicles and aircraft, and so on. This forms the basis of the skills necessary for industrialization.

The world-wide diffusion of this advanced technology creates a 'logic of industrialism', since it sets up a range of tasks and problems. The pressures towards efficient production will ensure that the most effective ways of tackling these common tasks inevitably become adopted world wide. As this process continues, organizations tackling the same tasks, in whichever culture, will become more and more alike.

As an example, let us imagine that we decide to go into business together to produce motor cars efficiently somewhere (anywhere) in the world. We know immediately that we must have factories of considerable size (individual craftsmen will not do), specialized machinery (hand tools or even general-purpose presses will not be sufficient by themselves), and supplies of raw materials (provided through specialist technical processes different from ours). Then we need trained people, expert in their particular tasks, to contribute a wide range of specialist knowledge, skills and effort. Last, but by no means least, we need professional managers who can raise and use capital to bring all these factors together and put them to work.

So, inevitably, with the spread of industrial technology goes a structure of industries. For motor cars we need a supply of steel, tyres, paint, upholstery, each of which in turn will have its own specialist processes and experts who complement our industry. The industrial structure becomes transformed from small craft units showing little technical specialization to a complex structure of large specialized units operating in an interdependent multi-organizational system. This system in turn leads to a particular division of labour. Rather than someone who can make sheet steel and rubber tyres and reinforced glass, we would prefer increased skill in only one of those tasks.

We also need people who can do production control, systems analysis, cost accounting, and so on, since these tasks too will be assigned to trained specialists in order to improve performance. So we will develop training in both technical and managerial tasks, and if we want a job done we will, in principle, appoint the person who by ability or training can do it best – regardless of colour, caste, tribe, religion, family or sex. Thus there will be greater social mobility (as we promote on merit) and physical mobility (as we expect everybody to move to where the workplace is). Not all of these changes can be achieved smoothly without conflict. So we will see the development of trade unions, collective bargaining, and a system of legal constraints.

All this was happening in the developed West from the turn of the century onwards. This does not mean that the process is completed – there are still many aspects of the idealized description given above that have not completely come to pass. For example, few countries in the world can claim they have completely effective policies on equal opportunities employment and promotion for all their ethnic sub-groups. But the developments are in this direction. These same processes can be seen happening now as the industrial technology reaches new countries, most notably in the Pacific rim. Within the last 30 years, for example, South Korea has established its own motor-manufacturing industry and is treading the industrialization path, being pushed by the need for efficiency into the same technology, expertise, training, organizational structure, and so on, as the others.

The convergence view does not mean that the traffic is necessarily all one way from the more developed to the less developed nations – although the main weight of transfer will clearly be in this direction. But contributions to effectiveness can come the other way too and will be incorporated into the world-wide way of doing things. For example, Japan was a late developer into industrialization, although the Japanese took to it very well when it came. They put a heavier emphasis on training workers. (This is part of a general Japanese cultural emphasis on education and training – Japanese children at age four plus are coached for entry to well-thought-of primary schools.) In the motor industry there has been much greater emphasis on training workers to produce parts and vehicles to highly reliable quality standards. This investment has paid off in terms of reliable products with a considerable competitive edge in the market, together with low rates of scrap and reduced costs of reworking during manufacture. The concept of quality control circles, was, in fact, conceived by a US professor, W. Edwards Deming, but he could not interest US managers in it. He presented his ideas in Japan, and they caught on very quickly, being more congruent with Japanese culture of full participation and discussion on operational issues. The Japanese have done so well out of this emphasis on quality that there is hardly a motor manufacturer in the West that has not instituted quality control circles in an effort to achieve the same benefits. They have now been widely adopted via the Total Quality Management movement into the global management convergence.

What else is going to be integrated into the world-wide convergence of methods of manufacturing motor cars? Well, as we saw in Section 1.2, Volkswagen in Germany has introduced the 'four day' week to avoid redundancies. This innovation fits in well with the characteristically 'structured' nature of German industrial culture with its emphasis on forward planning and worker consultation (Ebster-Grosz and Pugh, 1995). So particular management innovations will be inaugurated in cultures in which they are more likely to flourish, but if they are shown to give competitive advantage there, the ideas will then be taken seriously elsewhere, in spite of less cultural congruence.

2.2   THE MODERN INDUSTRIAL STATE

This section follows the arguments of J. K. Galbraith (1978). The traditional view of economic activity is the behaviour of buyers and sellers being regulated by the market through which the stimulus of competition is provided. Economic power is denied to any one person or firm because of price competition. But this system depends both on the existence of a large number of producers of a good or service, none of whom is in a position to dominate the market, and on a large number of buyers who individually are not large enough to affect the market.

This is clearly not the situation in modern industrial states, as Galbraith forcefully points out. Instead there is a process of mergers and take-overs by which the typical industry passes from a stage with many firms competing to a situation of a few large firms only – 'oligopoly' in economists' terms. As industrialization develops, bringing with it more and more sophisticated technology, the need for the large-scale corporations to control the market increases, since their investment is growing hugely and must be protected. Once time and money are invested (and products are taking longer to get to the market with greater technological sophistication – in the aviation industry, for example, decades rather than years) there is a great deal of inflexibility; it becomes very difficult to back out. Technology needs specialist experts who must be trained and managed. All this underlines the need to reduce the uncertainties involved, which means planning to control the market and insulate the corporation from it. Monopoly of supply or a guaranteed customer is aimed for. Both these options involve increasing state intervention.

The management of demand for the products of high-technology industries is more and more a matter for the state, through its attempts to establish control of the wage price spiral, its control of personal and corporate income tax, and its own role as a consumer. The net result is an increasing similarity in industrial societies in terms of the structure of capital, the elaborate organization and sophisticated technology which lead to the dominance of large corporations dependent on the state. Only in this way can the planning required for modern technology take place. Originally, this argument was applied to the developed West but now this form of governmental intervention, not always officially admitted, takes place in all countries with large capital investment, including, for example, Japan and Malaysia.

We have now looked at several pressures towards convergence in organizational forms: the processes of industrialization, the logic of rational efficiency, the specialist expertise and the training that industrialization requires, the diffusion of improved technical processes and procedures, large capital investment leading to the need for planning to replace the market, the increasing complexity of multi-organization structures, and the considerable involvement of the government. All of these push organizations along the route of planning and organizing in the same way. In the next sections we shall consider some more detailed characteristics of organizations and ask how they vary in different cultures.

2.3 THE GLOBAL PERVASIVENESS OF HIERARCHY

An approach to the analysis of organizational behaviour that has been carried out world wide is that of Tannenbaum and his colleagues (Tannenbaum, 1986). They use a framework of asking all members of an organization how much influence on the running of that organization various groups within it have. A wide range of groups can be investigated, but the simplest formulation has been to focus on the three levels of managers, supervisors and workers. Replies are made on a 5-point scale from 'little or no influence' to 'a very great deal of influence'. The mean scores for each group are then plotted to generate a characteristic diagram called a control graph. A hypothetical, but typical, example is given in Figure 3.

In the figure, the slope of the lines for company A (actual) and company B (actual) indicates the hierarchical distribution of influence and control. It shows a sharp reduction in control from one level to the next down the hierarchy, according to the views of members. This slope is present in all organizations. What does differ though is the gradient of the slope. It is steeper in Italian manufacturing firms than in US ones, demonstrating that the relative influence of higher levels is greater in Italy. It is flatter, but still exists, in 'self-managed enterprises' of the former Yugoslavia and in Israeli kibbutzim. In voluntary organizations (for example, trade unions, political parties) the lower levels have more influence, as they do in organizations staffed by professionals.

Clearly, differences in influence according to level in the hierarchy occur in a large variety of cultures and types of organizations, although the amount of the differences will vary. Furthermore, Tannenbaum asks members or organizations what the relative amount of influence should

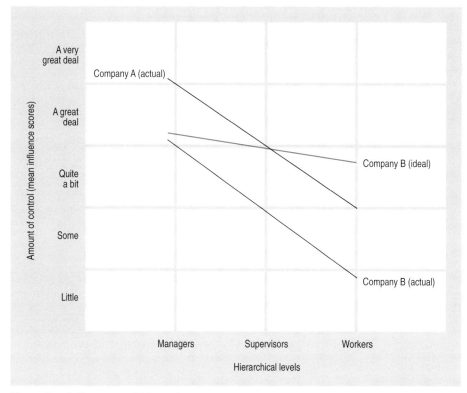

Figure 3   Influence and hierarchy

be across the levels. This generates an 'ideal' slope, as shown in Figure 3 for company B, which is typically less steep than the actual slope, reflecting the belief of many employees at lower levels that they themselves should have more say in what is going on. But the slope does not flatten completely, much less tip the other way. Few members of organizations suggest other than that upper levels should have more control than lower ones.

Tannenbaum argues that even within a hierarchical framework it is possible to increase the influence of lower levels because control is not a 'zero-sum game'. Thus both managers and workers can be rated as having greater influence, as in company A in Figure 3 where all levels are shown to have higher influence than their equivalents in company B. Tannenbaum advocates that this should be the way forward for greater effectiveness. He presents evidence that in Japanese mining and manufacturing companies, for example, all levels have a greater amount of influence than their equivalents in US concerns. Even so, the pervasive existence and acceptance of hierarchy would appear to be an important structural and operational basis for the global convergence of managerial processes.

2.4 ORGANIZATIONAL CONTEXT AND STRUCTURE IN VARIOUS CULTURES

In this section we shall examine the evidence for the pressures for convergence, based on the findings of an international research programme which has studied a large number of firms in a large number of countries. The studies are usually referred to as the Aston Programme of Research since they were inaugurated in the early 1960s at the University of Aston in Birmingham by Derek Pugh (now of the Open University Business School) and David Hickson (now of the University of

Bradford Management Centre). After initial studies in the UK, the researches were then carried out with colleagues in many other countries. The data thus form a useful comparative base on which to investigate the degree of organizational convergence internationally (Pugh, 1998).

The Aston studies set out to measure, in a comparative way, the degree of specialization of roles in a firm's structure. Organizations vary from those which have a highly differentiated set of specialist roles (for example, specialists in marketing, market research, advertising and public relations) to those in which these activities are carried out – probably only in a rudimentary way – by a more generalist sales manager. By asking a set of standard questions, the Aston researchers were able to calculate a comparative numerical score for each organization which characterizes it on the specialization dimension.

A second dimension of organization structure measured was formalization. How far and in what detail should we specify – particularly in writing – the work that people have to do, and how far do we allow them to use their own initiative to see what contribution they can make? F. W. Taylor (1912, reprinted in Pugh, 1997) was the high priest of formalization and standardization, and it was the motor industry which took his views to the furthest degree. Again, by asking a set of standard questions about the existence of documents and formal procedures, the Aston researchers were able to calculate a comparative numerical score for each organization which characterizes it on the formalization dimension.

A third major dimension of organization structure, which is concerned with the tension between hierarchy and participation, is centralization. In a highly centralized organization more of a standard list of decisions are taken higher up the hierarchy than in a less centralized organization which delegates the authority for more decisions lower down and thus allows greater participation.

Equipped with these measures, the Aston group were able to make a detailed comparative mapping of the structure of over 100 organizations. They then analysed the relationship of each organization's structure to the context in which it functioned. The context aspects that were studied included ownership patterns, number of employees, purpose (for example, product or service), the technology of the work processes, and the dependence of the organization on customers, suppliers, trade unions, and owning group.

They found some very clear relationships. The technical details can be found in Pugh (1998). We will summarize them briefly as follows.

- Size is strongly related to specialization and formalization.
- Size is related to decentralization.
- Parent group size is related to specialization and formalization.
- Technology has a definite but small relationship to specialization.
- Dependence is related to centralization.

Following on the studies in the UK, members of the Aston team with new collaborators in many different countries have used the approach to characterize the structures of over 1000 organizations, mainly manufacturing organizations, all over the world. There have been comparable studies in the USA, Canada, Germany, Sweden, Poland, Egypt, Jordan, India, Japan, Hungary, Brazil, Finland, and more.

There are many differences in the structures of organizations in different countries. Does that mean, therefore, that different cultures by their nature produce different organizational structures? Not necessarily. Let us take some examples.

The average specialization and formalization scores of the organizations studied in Jordan are less than half those in the UK sample. Does this mean that it is Jordanian culture that requires generalists to act informally? Before jumping to this conclusion let us consider the sizes of the organizations in the two samples. In Jordan, since it is a newly industrializing country, the organizations are much smaller (mean size 234 employees, range 30–1511) than in the UK sample (mean size 3411 employees, range 284–25,052). But we know that size is strongly related to specialization and formalization. So maybe the low specialization and formalization are due not to the particular Jordanian culture but to the smaller size of the organizations. This supposition can be tested quite directly because, if it is true, *within Jordan*, although the overall level is less, the relationship between size and specialization will be the same as within the UK. Larger Jordanian organizations will be more specialized and formalized than smaller ones. This is, in fact, the case.

The Aston research in Poland shows that firms there are considerably more centralized than the UK sample (average score over 50 per cent greater). Does this mean that there is something in the Polish culture that is conducive to centralized authority? Not necessarily. When this research was carried out Poland was a communist, centrally planned, economy; organizations there had a much higher degree of dependence on suppliers, customers, the state, and so on. If this is the reason for the high centralization, then again we would find that within Poland at that time, although the overall level was greater, the relationship between dependence and centralization was the same as within the UK. Thus more dependent Polish organizations will be more centralized than less dependent ones. This relationship was, indeed, found.

The same comparisons have been made for all the countries studied, and it is clear that there are considerable stabilities in the relationships found. Thus, within all these countries, bigger organizations are likely to have structures with more types of specialists and more formalization (and this effect is increased if they are part of larger owning groups). Companies more dependent on the owning groups for money and services, and more tied in to particular suppliers and customers, are likely to be more centralized and to lose autonomy. They are also likely to be more formalized in their procedures.

These relationships form a framework for understanding how organizations function world wide. Organizations converge because of the nature of the impact of the environmental context in which they operate. In all countries bigger organizations are more specialized and formalized in structure because everywhere growth means reaping economies of scale and more expertise as tasks are divided further. As specialists with their limited knowledge outnumber generalists, formalized methods are required for control: informal customs are inadequate to control large numbers of personnel. This process is accelerated where there is a large owning group, because the organization will develop specialists as counterparts to head office specialisms, and will take over group procedures and documentation.

Also, in all the countries studied, organizations that are more dependent on others in their environment take decisions centrally and lose autonomy to, say, a controlling board or ministry. This is because ties of ownership or contract are so important that the relevant resource decisions must be taken at the top. For example, if an enterprise purchases components from many different suppliers, decisions on each contract, including price, can be decentralized to the buying department, for some items even to junior buyers. But a contract for a year's supply of the major raw material is likely to require the chief executive's attention, thus leading to greater centralization. Dependent enterprises will also probably take on the formalization of other units to which they are linked.

The uniformity of these processes happening in all the countries studied is quite striking. Size and dependence become the bases for an explanation of the broad features of organizations world wide. It appears to be more important to know how large an organization is, who set it up, and what its dependence on the environment is, than where it is located. Certainly, the differences between organizations within one country are greater than the average differences between countries. For example, in spite of the different general levels, the most formalized Jordanian organization is much more formalized than the least formalized UK enterprise. And the least centralized Polish firm is considerably less centralized than the most centralized Japanese one.

As far as the context/structure relationship goes there would thus appear to be a clear convergence in all countries so far studied. But does it have to be like this? Is there a culture where these relationships do not hold, a country in which as organizations get bigger they get less formalized, or as they increase their dependence they decentralize? It is very difficult to imagine what sort of a culture this might be, and this very failure of imagination underlines the fact that finding one would be a major limitation of the convergence thesis.

2.5 PRODUCT GLOBALIZATION

A key factor pushing towards convergence is the trend towards globalization of products. There has been an enormous global communications explosion. People can see via television what is happening all over the world and this is shaping their aspirations. How many male teenagers in the world, for example, given the choice would now prefer to wear some form of characteristic national dress rather than t-shirts, jeans and trainers?

Usunier (1996) suggests four factors which push towards international product standardization:

- world-wide standards are converging in many industries, for example, oil drilling, nuclear engineering
- some products achieve international usage, for example, portable computers, high-tech manufactured products, duty-free articles, jeans
- innovative products are now launched globally, for example, laser disks, pharmaceutical innovations like Viagra
- markets are becoming less distinctive and more homogenized, for example, what were once distinctive national foods (hamburger, Chinese food, pizzas, curries) are now available all over the world – with some relatively slight variations for local tastes. (Who offers the 'genuine' pizza and where is often the subject of heated debate!)

The trend towards product globalization has brought economies of global scale in production, significant learning effects in service systems (for example, McDonalds operations over the world) and the power of global brands. These will all encourage a concomitant convergence in management functioning.

2.6   ENGLISH AS *THE* INTERNATIONAL LANGUAGE

A final factor which must be considered in the push towards global convergence is the acceptance of English as *the* international language. Anglo-Dutch Shell has been using English as its management language for over 70 years. But now, English is by far the most popular second language learnt all over the world. International Air Traffic Control works in English. Board meetings of Swedish multinationals such as ABB and Scania are conducted in English. In Germany, Siemens and Commerzbank use English for executive meetings and minutes. It has been estimated that three-quarters of the world's mail (post) is in English, and well over 80 per cent of the data stored on computers. The effect of this use of a common language will be to bring management procedures and understandings closer together.

Of course this 'international' English which is being developed is an 'artificial' language developed for convenience and related to the mother tongues of those that speak it. It is not the same as the English which native speakers talk. Native English is far more idiomatic, flexible, rich in metaphor, and therefore difficult for non-natives to understand. Guy and Mattock (1993) quote a Frenchman brandishing an English tabloid newspaper and asking 'You tell me this is a popular newspaper ... Why do I find it more difficult to read than *The Economist?*' This underlines a difficulty that native English speakers should be aware of: they are, in fact, at a disadvantage if they assume that the English they talk is the 'international version'.

For those who would like to explore this issue further, an extract from Guy and Mattock, 'Offshore English', is included in the Supplemental Readings Book.

2.7   CONCLUSION

We have now reviewed some of the arguments and evidence for world-wide convergence in the structure and functioning of companies. The arguments rely on: the logic of industrialism; the inevitable involvement of governments in the control of markets; and the effects of contextual characteristics (such as scale of operation and dependence on the environment) on the management structure of organizations in all cultures so far studied. The pervasive existence of a hierarchy of influence and control, and its general acceptance, has also been noted, as has the clear impact of product globalization. The evidence in support of a convergence in these aspects of organizational operations is considerable, but there are still large parts of management which remain distinctive for each country.

3 SYSTEMATIC CULTURAL DIFFERENCES AROUND THE WORLD

In Section 1 we examined some of the aspects of cultural differences that are likely to affect the operation of management. In this section we explore these differences further and see whether some systematic understanding of them can be developed. We shall start by examining the most comprehensive study of differences in work-related attitudes across the world, which was carried out in the 1970s.

IBM employees around the world

The Dutch social psychologist Geert Hofstede conducted a study based on two questionnaire surveys which produced a total of over 116,000 questionnaires from over 70 countries, making it by far the largest organization-based study ever to have been carried out. The respondents were all employees of IBM, the US multinational corporation which operates in most countries in the world. For greater comparability, only the sales and service employees of IBM were considered.

The first analyses (Hofstede, 1980) were made only on data collected in the 39 countries of the larger subsidiaries, in each of which the IBM affiliate is staffed almost entirely by indigenous employees. (A Yugoslav self-managed organization was added; although not a subsidiary, it markets and services IBM products.) Within the sales and service department, all types of employee were surveyed – sales assistants, professional scientists, top managers, and so on – using the language of each country. Versions of the questionnaire in a total of 20 languages had to be made.

The design of the research enabled several factors to be controlled. All the respondents were doing the same tasks (selling and servicing IBM products) within the same general overall framework. Thus the technology, jobs and some formal procedures were the same. The respondents' age categories and sex composition were broadly similar (and where these factors were shown to be related to attitudes their effects were statistically adjusted for). Only the nationalities differed. The differences in attitudes and values could therefore be said to be related to cultural differences rather than organizational ones. Indeed Hofstede argues that the national cultural differences found within IBM are likely to be conservative underestimates of those existing within the countries at large. The survey was repeated with stable results, underlining the cultural nature of the differences found.

Activity 2

Please stop now and read the article 'The cultural relativity of organizational practices and theories', by Hofstede in the Reader. We shall be referring to it at various points during this section.

We shall quickly summarize various points that Hofstede makes and also elaborate on them. His work is an outstanding attempt to get a systematic classification of cultural differences. Systematic comparisons are important because otherwise we would have to learn an almost unending list of cultural characteristics every time we approached another culture. Classification, by examining similarities and differences between cultures, helps us to understand a new culture more quickly by placing it in an analytic framework.

Hofstede identifies four basic dimensions of the differences between national cultures. Each of the 40 national cultures can be rated from high to low on each of the four scales as shown in Table 1, and is thus given a distinctive classification.

Table 1 Hofstede's dimensions		
Dimension	**Rating**	
1 Power distance	Large (distant)	Small (close)
2 Uncertainty avoidance	Strong (risk avoiders)	Weak (able to tolerate ambiguity)
3 Individualism–collectivism	High (individualistic)	Low (collectivistic)
4 Masculinity–femininity	High (masculine)	Low (feminine)

3.1   THE POWER DISTANCE DIMENSION

Power distance is concerned with how far the culture encourages superiors to exert power. In a large power distance culture (for example, the Philippines, India) that is what being a boss means. Inequality is accepted: 'a place for everyone and everyone in their place'. Subordinates consider superiors to be different kinds of people; indeed, it is felt that those in power should try to look as powerful as possible. In addition there is latent conflict between the powerful and the powerless. Other people can rarely be trusted because they pose potential threats to one's power; having power over someone, and being dependent on someone, are the basis for collaboration.

In a small power distance culture (for example, Austria, Israel) superiors and subordinates consider each other to be colleagues and both believe that inequality in society should be minimized. So those in power should try to look less powerful than they are and, since a latent harmony exists, trust is possible. Superiors are accessible because organization members are interdependent.

Examples of the questions asked are given below.

POWER DISTANCE QUESTIONS

1   How frequently in your experience does the following problem occur: employees being afraid to express disagreement with their managers:

Very frequently/Frequently/Sometimes/Seldom/Very seldom

2   Which type of manager would you prefer to work for? One who:

– makes decisions and then tells staff

– makes decisions and explains reasons fully to staff

– consults with staff before making decisions.

(Hofstede, 1980, Appendix 1)

In large power distance cultures, employees are frequently afraid to express disagreement, and prefer to work for managers who take decisions (and responsibility) and then tell them what to do. In small power distance cultures, employees are seldom afraid to disagree, and expect to be consulted before decisions are made.

French and German factory comparisons

To explore the meaning of the power distance dimension, we shall now look at an important study comparing the management of French and West German factories. Maurice (1979) carried out a comparative study of the relative status and wage payments of workers and managers in similar factories in France and West Germany. In order to control (by screening out) factors such as size, industrial sector and technology, the researchers compared only factories in equivalent industries (such as iron and steel, paper and cardboard products) who used the same technology and were similar in size. They were thus able to focus on national differences in hierarchy, job structures and payments.

Their results showed clear differences between the French and German firms, including those given below.

1   There were considerably more staff not employed directly on physically making the product in French than in German firms, and they were relatively better paid.

2   The wage differential between the lowest and the highest paid of all employees was much greater in French than German firms. Indeed, the difference was such that there was no overlap: the largest differential found in a German firm was still less than the smallest differential found in a French firm (2.7 times as against 3.7).

3   The number of levels in the production hierarchy was greater in French than in German firms (5 compared with 3) because there were more middle-level managers in the French firms.

Maurice argues that these differences are not fortuitous but relate to differences in the educational systems of France and Germany. More top managers in France hold higher degrees, usually from the *grandes écoles*. These are very high-status university institutes which provide high-level technical and scientific education and which, by their very selective intake, provide an élite of high-status managers for French organizations. Graduates from the *grandes écoles* are recruited directly into the upper levels of firms and are paid relatively much greater salaries than in Germany. This means that there is a group of less qualified supervisors and managers who can expect to be promoted only through the middle ranks of the organization. They can never realistically aspire to join the top management set or *cadre*.

In Germany, equivalent top managers are often promoted from within the firm which they join lower down with fewer general and more technical qualifications. Thus at the lower levels German supervisors are better qualified and better paid than their French equivalents. They can also take more technical decisions and are given more professional autonomy.

In summary, the differences show that French firms are run more bureaucratically, with orders and procedures set from above, while German work organization relies more on professional expertise derived from the trained knowledge and skill of the more junior employees. Since these differences are well grounded in the educational systems of the two countries, their organizations are likely to be slow in converging and to resist pressures to become congruent even in the European Union.

Review Question 1 _____

From the comparative description that Maurice gives, would you regard French or German management as higher on the Hofstede power distance dimension? List some of the characteristics which led to your conclusion.

3.2 THE UNCERTAINTY AVOIDANCE DIMENSION

Hofstede's second dimension is the degree to which a culture copes with novelty and encourages risk taking. All organizations face environmental change and uncertainty and try to adapt to them. This is true in all countries, but Hofstede found a considerable range across cultures in people's attitudes to risk and abilities to tolerate uncertainty.

In a strong uncertainty avoidance culture (for example, Greece, Portugal) people feel threatened by uncertain situations and experience high anxiety and stress. This is combated by hard work, career stability and intolerance of deviancy. There is a search for ultimate values and a great respect for age. In a weak uncertainty avoidance culture (for example, Denmark, Hong Kong) the uncertainty inherent in life is more easily accepted and each day is taken as it comes – which means that less stress is experienced. The need for rules is less and a very pragmatic view is taken about keeping or changing those rules in existence.

Examples of the uncertainty avoidance questions are given below.

UNCERTAINTY AVOIDANCE QUESTIONS

1   Company rules should not be broken – even when employees think it is in the company's best interests

Strongly agree/Agree/Undecided/Disagree/Strongly disagree

2   How long do you think you will continue working for this company?

Till I retire/More than 5 years/2–5 years/Up to 2 years

(Hofstede, 1980, Appendix 1)

In strong uncertainty avoidance cultures, employees agree that rules should not be broken and look forward to staying with the firm until they retire.

Japanese work organization

To explore the meaning of the uncertainty avoidance dimension further we shall consider the functioning of Japanese organizations, using material from a number of research studies. Dore (1973) is a classic comparative study of Japanese and UK industrial relations systems. Ouchi (1981) is an examination by a Japanese-US academic of what US business can learn from Japanese organization, given that it cannot expect to adopt their practices completely. Ballon (1983) is a penetrating analysis by a French Jesuit priest who has been professor of management at a Japanese (Christian) university for many decades. In addition, the discussion draws on conversations with a number of visiting Japanese professors of management, including Professors Sasaki, Okamoto and Kono.

Since Japan's post World War II economic and industrial successes, a lot has been written about Japanese work organization, much of it with overtones of selling the 'miracle ingredient' to Western countries. But it is important to understand that Japanese organization stems from Japanese culture and its values.

The first important value is concerned with interdependence. The Japanese identify with their country. It is their destiny to be Japanese and alike in so many respects. Out of a population of over 115 million, only 700,000 are non-Japanese. (Compare this with the UK. For many in the UK the identification as English, Scottish, Welsh or Irish is as important as the British identification. In addition, 6.6 per cent of the usually resident population were born abroad – over ten times the Japanese percentage.) In public opinion surveys in Japan, 90 per cent of respondents identify themselves as belonging to the middle class. Their second identification is in terms of work – not, as it would be in the West, by what work they do (trade, profession, skill), but by where they do it. The Japanese term for workplace means much more than the physical location. A Japanese who tells you that they work in the Hitachi company at the Taga factory is telling you much more than an English person who says they work for GEC at Rugby. The Japanese is giving you an identification of himself or herself in the eyes of society – the nearest British analogy is with the armed services or the police force.

A result of this degree of identification is that the members of a work organization look upon their goals and those of the organization as being fundamentally in agreement. As they see it, the survival of the organization is necessary for their own survival, so the difference between owners and workers is not an overriding consideration or a barrier to motivation. The achievement of success benefits everybody: shareholders, managers, workers, customers, suppliers, the government. Everyone is working towards the same goal, so egalitarian work practices mark the approach. Managers, engineers and workers wear the same uniform, eat in the same canteen, work the same hours. Offices are open plan, with everybody participating and aware of what is going on. Superiors are in direct and constant interactions with their subordinates, and everyone can actually see what the informal interaction system is and who is influential.

This degree of identification is possible because the norm, in large organizations, is permanent employment. It is a life process: organizational birth (entering the company on leaving school or university), ageing (building up seniority, experience and wisdom) and death (mandatory retirement at 55 years old). This norm helps us to understand the Japanese view of their organizations, although it operates only in the large organizations, covering perhaps 40 per cent of the *male* workforce. It does not apply to smaller organizations who do not have the economic stability to retain workers in the face of falling revenue; neither does it apply to women workers, who are expected to leave on marriage. Although women may return when the children have started full-time schooling, they are regarded as temporary and are used as a buffer in work fluctuations.

Another component of the organizational identification is that unions are specific to the organization. About 30 per cent of employees are union members and over 90 per cent of these unions represent all the workers in an enterprise up to the level of manager. 'Blue-collar' and 'white-collar' workers in the same firm belong to the same union. In a university, professors, technicians and catering personnel belong to the same union. The principle is 'one enterprise, one union'. If the company goes out of business, so does the union. The union is thus committed to the development of the enterprise, while retaining a specific interest in the employment, security and development of its members. For example, unions support automation as a means of upgrading their members' jobs.

The second key Japanese cultural value is the respect and status given to age. We have already commented on this in the Introduction to the course. Japan is a 'gerontocracy', that is, ruled by the aged. Seniority – the Japanese use the term 'the merit of years' – is the basis of pay and promotion. The salary system is always complex and flexible. It has little to do with the work done as measured by job evaluation, piece rates and individual incentive bonuses. These are unacceptable because they could lead to younger people being paid more than older ones. The salary is based on (1) years of service (which correlates very closely with age), (2) qualifications obtained, and (3) a company-wide bonus based on the performance, not of the individual, but of the enterprise as a whole.

This bonus is quite considerable, up to one-third of salary. It thus increases the commitment of the employees to the success of the firm, since they have a large financial stake in it. It also helps to maintain the lifetime employment system, since in a bad year a firm could pay a small bonus or even forgo it altogether, thus saving, say, a quarter of the labour costs without the need for any redundancies. It would then be in a good position to expand when required in a later year. In good years the bonuses are high and employees save them; the rate of capital formation in Japan has been estimated at four times that of the USA. In economic terms such a bonus scheme transfers part of the entrepreneurial risks of the business from the shareholders to the employees, who take the risks and get the benefits. No wonder nearly all the Japanese regard themselves as middle class.

One important effect of this method of payment is that it is not necessary to define roles or jobs very precisely. This means that organization structures are 'softer'. A person will be appointed to a department, not necessarily with a specific job title or description, and will be expected to do whatever is required. So there is considerably greater overlap among jobs, a much greater emphasis on communication, and decision making by consensus. The 'softness' of the organization means that there is intentional ambiguity about who is responsible for which decision, since this encourages joint responsibility. As a result, decisions take longer to make, but what matters for a Japanese manager is not the decision but the implementation. From his point of view – there are hardly any Japanese women managers yet – an ideal decision is one where, after there has been full discussion with all concerned about the implementation of possible options, the decision (and the commitment to implementation) takes itself. This form of collective responsibility is known as the practice of *ringi.* As a physical manifestation of this generation of commitment, a document proposing a change (the *ringi-sho*) may typically show the seals of approval of 20 or more managers before the director puts his final seal on it.

There are also costs associated with the very considerable commitment shown. The *ringi* system can take a long time and can degenerate into time wasting with people becoming involved just to be seen to be involved. The process clearly fosters conformity through social pressures since the more who signify consent the more difficult it is *not* to concur. Political corruption also, when it is for the good of the company, is not easily resisted. 'Whistle blowing', hard enough in any culture, is even harder here, since it involves illegitimate challenge to the accepted system. The procedures can then become a form of collective *ir*responsibility.

One final important cultural value in Japan is the high respect for education. This includes technical training, on-the-job training, and management development. The way up through the organization is by training and experience. Managers are moved around to different departments, and most managers have worked on the factory shop-floor. Workers learn all the jobs carried out in their section in order to increase flexibility of working. Their role is not just to follow instructions from the supervisors. Their task is to see that the equipment contributes optimally to the production process. They are concerned with maintenance and with quality (through quality control circles), and they contribute to suggestion schemes at a rate 100 times greater than in the UK or the USA. However, Japanese employees do not appear to show great satisfaction with these work systems. They make more complaints than UK or US workers. Since work is so closely integrated into their lives, they have high aspirations and continually see things which should be improved.

But as we noted in Section 1.1, cultures are continually changing. The impact of world-wide economic fluctuations on all cultures, together with the global communications revolution means that changes will inevitably take place. The second class status of women on which the traditional Japanese managerial culture depends is being eroded as higher educational standards for women and higher career aspirations for them are developing apace. Such foundations of the Japanese culture as respect for authority and undying commitment to one particular employer are weakening. Younger workers now report dissatisfaction with hierarchies based on age rather than knowledge and skill. In order to survive in a tough global economic climate, employers are having to make many more workers redundant. At the time of writing (1998) the Japanese Government is considering introducing mechanisms to make mobility in the labour market easier by weakening the currently very strong unfair dismissal laws. But there will, of course, be considerable opposition and it may take some time. Although cultures change, they do so slowly.

Review Question 2

From the description given above, would you consider that the culture of Japanese work organizations is strong or weak on the Hofstede uncertainty avoidance dimension? List the characteristics which led you to your conclusion.

3.3 THE INDIVIDUALISM–COLLECTIVISM DIMENSION

The individualism–collectivism dimension is the degree to which a culture encourages individual as opposed to collectivist or group concerns. In an individualistic culture (for example, the USA, the UK) identity is based on the individual. The emphasis is on individual initiative and achievement, and one is supposed to take care of oneself plus only the immediate family. Everybody has the right to a private life and opinion, and may well have only a calculating or instrumental involvement with work. A collectivist culture (for example, Iran, Hong Kong) is characterized by a tighter social framework, where people are members of extended families or clans which protect them in exchange for loyalty. The emphasis is on belonging and the aim is to be a good member – whereas in the individualist culture the ideal is to be a good leader. The collectivist involvement with the work organization is a moral one, and there is a belief in group decisions. The value standards applied to members of one's own group, clan or organization can differ considerably from those applied to others.

Some sample questions are given below.

INDIVIDUALISM QUESTIONS

1   How important is it for you to have a job which leaves you sufficient time for your personal or family life?

Of utmost importance/Very important/Of moderate importance/Little importance/Very little or no importance

2   How important to you are training opportunities to improve your skills or to learn new skills?

Of utmost importance / Very important / Of moderate importance /Little importance /Very little or no importance

(Hofstede, 1980, Appendix 1)

In an individualist culture it is very important to have time for personal and family life, and not very important to have job training, since it increases commitment to the company. In a collectivist culture the opposite views hold: employees value good physical working conditions and find personal challenge in work of little importance.

Arab executives

To explore the meaning of the individualism–collectivism dimension we shall consider the management style of a typical Arab business executive. The economic impact of the Arab world with its oil-based wealth has led to the growing importance of Arab business executives (as distinct from Arab traders, who have a commercial tradition that dates back many centuries). An executive directs and is responsible for the operations of a manufacturing or service business which may be owned privately or by the government. Muna (1980) conducted a survey of a number of leading Arab executives – all men, for few women have entered this sphere yet. He asked them about their practices and their views on the nature of management.

If you come to do business with an Arab executive, Muna reports, he will invariably engage in social talk for what seems, to a Westerner, a long time. After you have partaken of drinks (coffee, tea or soft drinks, of course) there will then be a period of up to 15 minutes when you and the executive talk about several topics of interest, provided that they are not to do with the business in hand. It would be regarded as impolite and rather shocking to start immediately with a business discussion..This ritual might seem to be merely a quaint survival from more spacious days. In fact, it is one particular manifestation of a very important value that runs throughout Arab society.

The value concerns the importance given to personal relationships as distinct from role- or task-oriented ones. In the Arab culture, it matters who you are – not just what your job is. The conversation is to allow exploration on a person-to-person basis, to establish interpersonal trust, to evaluate you as a person and to locate you precisely in the business, national and family network. If you are already known, the talking cements and builds on the relationship. Arab executives dislike impersonal, role-based, or transient relationships when something as important as business activity is involved.

This means that there can be no basic separation of business affairs from social or personal life. Executives are on call from employees, clients or government officials, at home and over the weekends – precisely because these people are not just employees, clients or officials, but individuals with whom a relationship has been built up. Arab managers run an open-door policy: any employee can come with a problem to the top executive, and there is a low level of delegation of decisions, although consultation and discussion take place before the decision is made. Friends will drop in at the office for chats over coffee, drawing on the personal relationship and its concomitant norm of hospitality. Even though he has work to do, it would be unethical for an executive to refuse to see visitors. Loyalty and trust are rated much more highly than efficiency in performance.

There is a strong kinship structure in all parts of Arab society, based on the clan in tribal communities and the extended family in rural and urban milieu. So what we in the West would call 'nepotism' is right and proper, and executives accept that they have a duty to hire relatives in their organizations. They use family (and are used by them) as contacts and lobbyists with other organizations and government departments, to expedite, advance and influence the course of events in their favour. It is, of course, a give-and-take process and the executive will have in his mind a balance sheet of credits and debits of favours given and taken, for each of his relationships.

Money can also enter into this balance, and paying money for favours does not have the same connotations of bribery as it does in a systematic procedure-oriented culture. From the Arab point of view, everybody is 'bribing' everybody else all the time after all. That is how the personal relationships are nourished. Since these attitudes and behaviours are so integrated into Arab culture, it is argued that Arab managers will long behave differently from, say, Western ones.

Review Question 3 _____

Would the Arab executive culture be high or low on the Hofstede individualism–collectivism dimension? List the characteristics which lead you to your conclusion.

High-context and low-context speech

There is an important further distinction between cultures in addition to those on Hofstede's list. This is in the way language is used, as described by Hall (1976), where he differentiates between high-context speech and low-context speech. In a low-context culture the aim is for the message to be as explicit as possible. How the message is put will depend relatively little on the context in which it is given. It will primarily be conveyed by the words spoken. In a high-context culture the spoken words indicate the message implicitly, but convey only a small portion of it. It would be regarded as crass, uncouth and impolite if account were not taken of the previous knowledge of the recipient, the relationships between the participants, and other aspects of the context in which the message is delivered. You do not refuse your guests directly, for example. Words like 'maybe', 'perhaps', 'we'll consider it', if uttered in a high-context culture to a foreigner are likely to be polite ways of refusing. Table 2 gives examples of languages that Hall considers to be of high and low context.

Table 2 High- and low-context languages		
	High-context languages	**Low-context languages**
Nature of communication	Implicit speech	Explicit speech
Group orientation	Collective	Individual
Languages	Japanese Arabic Chinese Latin American Spanish	German Swedish, Danish French North American English

(Source: adapted from Hall, 1976)

It has been pointed out that there is a good correlation between the Hall notion of high and low context and the Hofstede dimension of individualism. Countries high on individualism have lower-context speech. They will be more direct, succinct, have more references to 'I', and likely to spell out specific goals. High-context, collectivist cultures will be more discursive, refer to 'we', and have more qualifying words – 'maybe', 'perhaps', 'probably' – and the speaker will look for reactions from the listener and tailor the speech accordingly.

Learning these distinctions is an important part of becoming effective in cross-cultural communications. It is necessary for managers to find out the nature of the culture in which they operate. Remember, though, that descriptions such as those given here inevitably involve a considerable degree of summary and compression. The most obvious example is regarding each country as a homogeneous culture, even though this is not always the case. For example, Italian is not listed in the box above because there are major differences between the individualistic north of Italy and the collectivist south.

One study intriguingly demonstrated the north–south divide in Italy by comparing the types of insult used. Northern Italians use more individualist insults, while Southerners use relational and collectivist insults. To help you know how to insult appropriately in Italy should the occasion arise, here are some examples:

ITALIAN INSULTS

Individualist insults of Northern Italy

You are stupid

You are a cretin

Swear words referring to religious figures

Swear words referring to sexual organs

Collectivist insults of Southern Italy

I wish a cancer on you and all your relatives

Your sister is a cow

You are queer and so is your father

Insults relating to incest

(Adapted from Semin and Rubini, 1990)

3.4 THE MASCULINITY–FEMININITY DIMENSION

Hofstede calls the final dimension of differentiation between cultures 'masculinity' at one end to contrast with 'femininity' at the other. These dimensions are, perhaps, unfortunately named, because they take a Western stereotype of the roles of masculinity and femininity. At the 'masculine' end of the dimension the emphasis is on the achievement of tasks, winning rather losing, with much less regard to the 'costs' of such achievement. The 'feminine' end shows concern for the whole context and process, and looks for ways of satisfying many participants' goals. In cultures that score high on masculinity (for example, Australia, Italy) performance is what counts. Money and material standards are important, ambition is the driving force. Big and fast are beautiful, 'machismo' is sexy.

Conversely, in cultures that score high on 'femininity' (for example, the Netherlands, Sweden) it is the quality of life that matters, people and the environment are important, service provides the motivation, small is beautiful, and unisex is attractive. As may be expected, a major difference between the cultures at the two ends of this dimension is the relationship of men and women. In 'masculine' cultures the sex roles are clearly differentiated. Men should be assertive, dominating; women should be caring, nurturing. A dominant woman is regarded as unfeminine, although she can influence in the background. In 'feminine' cultures the sex roles are more flexible, and there is a belief in equality between the sexes. It is not 'unmasculine' for a man to take a caring role.

Below are some questions that are important in determining a culture's masculinity score.

MASCULINITY–FEMININITY QUESTIONS

How important is it to you to:

1 Have an opportunity for high earnings?

Utmost importance/Very/Moderate/Little/Very little or no importance

2 Work with people who co-operate well with one another?

Utmost importance/Very/Moderate/Little/Very little or no importance

(Hofstede, 1980, Appendix 1)

It is very important in a 'masculine' culture to have an opportunity for high earnings but of little importance to work with a co-operative group, while in a 'feminine' culture the reverse is the case for both these issues. In addition, a 'feminine' culture values living in a pleasant area, and puts less value on the need to get recognition from others for a good job done.

The British managerial culture

In this section we shall explore the masculinity–femininity dimension by considering British managerial culture from the point of view of how it strikes two US management academics. They both started from the premise that British management is failing as the UK falls behind in economic terms. Their views reflect their personal impressions, but since they formed and published these independently (Dubin, 1970; Steele, 1977) the amount of overlap in their comments is impressive. Below are some of the characteristics in which they see the British managers differing from US managers and which might be contributing to the UK's economic decline.

1 Perfectibility: doing better is a good thing

US managers believe that current ways of doing things will inevitably be replaced by even better things. They are optimists who consider that the future holds much promise, and are willing to change to discover better possibilities. British managers value security and continuity, and think that 'we must be doing all right now or we wouldn't be here'. (This is not necessarily true: the inadequacies may not have become critical – yet.) They are pessimists, well aware of the costs of change, and require proof that it will work before it is adopted. But proof can often be supplied only after the change is carried through. So innovations are much less likely in the UK than the USA.

2 Class position: the legitimacy of hierarchical authority

British managers can be characterized as middle-class men (and some women) who have had a 'proper' education. What is strange for Americans is that 'proper', in the British understanding, seems to be defined in terms of where you were educated, not what you studied. Recruiters are seen as more interested in the fact that the applicant went to public or grammar school than how many 'A' levels they obtained. They are more concerned that the candidate went to a 'good' university than with the class of degree. Of course, the children of working-class parents can get to university, qualify and be selected as managers – but by then they are middle class anyway. There is much less awareness in the UK than in the USA that at lower levels in the organization there is a pool of talented people who are quite capable of being developed into successful managers. In the UK they are neglected on class grounds, since they do not fit the supposed social requirements.

This waste carries on because there is a deep sense of the legitimacy of hierarchical authority in UK organizations, which stems from the class divisions. This is why the socially acceptable gifted amateur is regarded as much more desirable than the average professional for top positions.

3 Personal trust: the neglect of other forms of evaluation

British managers place much more emphasis than US managers on personal trust and loyalty in their subordinates. It is often the prime criterion in valuing them. 'Trust' does not just mean that they will not be found with a hand in the till – it is much more than that. It means that you trust them to be 'sound', to do 'the right thing' even in your absence; in fact, to think and act like you. The problem is that this sort of trust acts as a great pressure towards conformity, both in thought and action. Trustworthy subordinates rarely surprise their superiors with innovative actions – that would risk being regarded as 'unsound'.

The same process happens in the USA but to a much lower degree, because of the much greater emphasis on universalistic criteria both for selection and evaluation. In the USA these criteria are, to a much greater degree, independent of the particular views of the current boss. They are set for the organization as a whole in terms of operational and financial achievement. Universalistic criteria are necessary because there are more frequent job changes at all levels in US organizations. In theory the UK practice of personalizing the criteria should mean that exceptions are made for exceptionally good people who don't 'fit' as well as poor ones. But in practice the opposite is the case: a manager almost always has to call on personal criteria to justify retaining staff who are inadequate in terms of achievement or potential. This approach also relieves the boss of having to make the hard decisions to get rid of inadequate subordinates. In the USA the 'bottom line' of output produced, profit achieved, and so on, is more central to the evaluation.

For both Dublin and Steele, the implication of their analyses is that UK firms should become more like US ones in these respects. Otherwise the likelihood of adaptation and self-renewal is small. Indeed, successful firms are more 'American' in their practices.

Review Question 4 _____

(a) From the comparative descriptions that Dubin and Steele give, would you regard US or UK management as higher on the Hofstede 'masculinity' dimension? List some of the characteristics that lead you to your conclusion.

(b) Of course Dubin and Steele were reflecting on the UK industrial scene of the 1970s. Cultures do develop, as we have said, and you might like to reflect on whether in your experience things have changed as a result of the Thatcher and post-Thatcher eras. And in what way has management changed?

3.5 INTERPRETING THE DIMENSIONS

Equipped with measurements that locate the 40 cultures along the four dimensions, Hofstede then offers 'a set of cultural maps of the world'. The examples we have given are at the extremes of the dimensions. But you should not forget that the cultures are spread out along the scales from one end to the other, and the dimensions are not dichotomies. Cultures are not either masculine like Italy or feminine like Sweden, but there are many countries in-between: Belgium exactly in the centre, Britain on the masculine side, France on the feminine one. The same is true for uncertainty avoidance: Japan is very high on this dimension and Singapore is very low, but Thailand is in-between; so is West Germany compared with Greece (high) and Denmark (low). The same range exists for power distance: Mexico is high and Denmark is low, but Portugal and Taiwan are in the middle. On the individualism dimension, Spain and Finland are between New Zealand (high) and Pakistan (low).

3.6 CLASSIFYING CULTURES BY THE DIMENSIONS

Table 3 (overleaf) classifies the cultures according to the four dimensions, and assigns summary names. The 40 cultures are arranged in eight culture areas according to the statistical technique of cluster analysis. This technique forms the clusters by putting together cultures that are as like each other as possible while being as different as possible from the other groups. Remember that the clusters were formed from the answers to the questions on the four work values and the scores on the four dimensions calculated from them. The area names were given after the clusters had emerged from the analysis.

The first striking thing about this classification is that it does in general put together groups which appear to belong in geographical, linguistic and historical terms. The two obvious mismatches are Italy (put with the Germanic group) and Yugoslavia (put with the less developed Latin cluster). These issues need further research, but in general the relationship to historical development is most impressive. This gives the whole exercise conviction, since it is from these characteristics that we should expect work attitudes to derive. The second point is that the results suggest that culture really does matter in relation to work attitudes, since the differences are shown up so clearly and systematically.

There are some very clear relationships between the groups. High power distance unites the Latin and the Asian areas as against the Germanic, Anglo and Nordic ones. Uncertainty avoidance has quite a different pattern, linking Latin with Germanic and Near Eastern. Individualism is a characteristic of developed countries, while developing countries have a collective orientation. The Germanic and Anglo groups, with their high masculinity, differ sharply from the Nordic. Japan is in a group of its own, not being sufficiently close to any other culture in the study.

Of course some countries have developed since the 1970s when these studies were carried out. This is very strongly shown in the Pacific Rim. It is clear that Taiwan and Singapore (as we discuss in Section 3.8) have developed considerably in economic terms since then and would no longer be placed in Group IV of Table 3 as 'less developed Asian'. They have now moved into the more developed Asian Group III to join Japan. It will be interesting to see over the years how their cultures change as a result.

Table 3   Country clusters and their characteristics

I: More developed Latin

high power distance
high uncertainty avoidance
high individualism
medium masculinity

Belgium
France
Argentina
Brazil
Spain

II: Less developed Latin

high power distance
high uncertainty avoidance
low individualism
whole range on masculinity

Columbia
Mexico
Venezuela
Chile
Peru
Portugal
Yugoslavia (former)

III: More developed Asian

medium power distance
high uncertainty
  avoidance
medium individualism
high masculinity

Japan

IV: Less developed Asian

high power distance
low uncertainty
  avoidance
low individualism
medium masculinity

Pakistan
Taiwan
Thailand
Hong Kong
India
Philippines
Singapore

V: Near Eastern

high power distance
high uncertainty
  avoidance
low individualism
medium masculinity

Greece
Iran
Turkey

VI: Germanic

low power distance
high uncertainty
  avoidance
medium individualism
high masculinity

Austria
Israel
Germany
Switzerland
South Africa
Italy

VII: Anglo

low power distance
low to medium
  uncertainty avoidance
high individualism
high masculinity

Australia
Canada
Britain
Ireland
New Zealand
USA

VIII: Nordic

low power distance
low to medium
  uncertainty avoidance
medium individualism
low masculinity

Denmark
Finland
Netherlands
Norway
Sweden

(Source: adapted from Hofstede, 1980, p. 336)

3.7 IMPLICIT MODELS OF ORGANIZATION FUNCTIONING

Since a culture's work-related values are so distinctive and different, it is to be expected that the processes and behaviour of its organizations will be too. Hofstede argues very strongly that we should not expect the same conceptions about and prescriptions for management, for example, to be appropriate in all culture areas. They need to be culture-specific, since each culture group will have its own implicit model of organizational functioning. From their scores on the dimensions, we can discern the implicit model underlying how people from a certain culture group think about how organizations function; and therefore we can determine what would be appropriate management behaviour.

Hofstede suggests four very distinctive models.

1   The less developed Asian group, with its high power distance and low uncertainty avoidance, has an implicit model that an organization is like a family – it will cope with whatever comes along through the power of the leader or father figure.

2   The Germanic group (low power distance, high uncertainty avoidance) will look for ways of coping by designing rules and procedures which, if carried out, avoid the need for personal exercise of power; the implicit model here is a well-oiled machine.

3   For the Anglo group (low power distance, low to medium uncertainty avoidance) the implicit model is a market, in which coping is achieved flexibly by continuous bargaining among members.

4   For the Latin and Near Eastern groups (high power distance, high uncertainty avoidance) both the power relationships and the work processes are prescribed, and the implicit organizational model is a human pyramid.

Hofstede concludes that we should not expect convergence of leadership styles or management practices across these different cultural forms, since they are dependent on the implicit model of organizational functioning prevalent in the particular culture. The models in turn are generated by the mental programming to which the culture into which we are born exposes us from birth. Changes in culture are inevitably, therefore, very slow.

3.8   THE LONG-TERM DIMENSION

If, as Hofstede argues, culture is so important in affecting the way everybody thinks, then it must also affect the theories which scholars propose, for they are part of their own culture. So, for example, theories about culture itself will be affected. Hofstede's own background is Western European. Indeed, most research questionnaires on culture are developed and used by Westerners. Is all this research therefore culture-biased, and has this bias affected the four dimensions discussed above which Hofstede has developed and applied to organizational value systems? Do the dimensions miss essential aspects of, say, Eastern organizations and management, by not asking the right questions?

Hofstede had been concerned about this issue, and one of his collaborators carried out an innovative attempt to circumvent the problem by starting from a different base. Michael Harris Bond (a Canadian, living and working in Hong Kong) wanted to develop a questionnaire which, if it was biased, would have an Eastern bias not a Western one. So he asked Chinese social scientists in Hong Kong and Taiwan to specify a list of Chinese values. From these, a questionnaire was constructed in Chinese and then translated into English and eight other languages – the opposite way from the usual sequence. The questionnaire was given to a range of students in 23 countries (Hofstede and Bond, 1988).

Four cultural dimensions emerged in the analysis. One was similar to power–distance (Section 3.1 above) but with an Asian emphasis on moderation in the use of authority conferred by status. A second was concerned with masculinity–femininity (Section 3.4 above) but with an Asian emphasis on courteously restraining over-assertiveness. A third exemplified the individualism–collectivism dimension (Section 3.3 above). These three dimensions seem to refer to values about choices fundamental to the management-related elements of all cultures. They are the attitudes to authority, to others, and to managing yourself in relation to the task, which we discussed in Section 1.3 above. They show an encouraging stability (for convergence theorists) on issues which are relevant in all cultures.

But the fourth 'Western' dimension of uncertainty avoidance (Section 3.2 above) did not appear in the analysis. It was replaced by a dimension which contrasted the greater importance of:

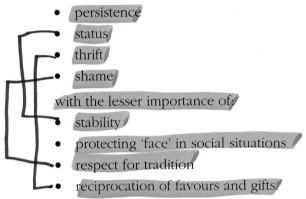

- persistence
- status
- thrift
- shame

with the lesser importance of:

- stability
- protecting 'face' in social situations
- respect for tradition
- reciprocation of favours and gifts.

All the values expressed in this dimension come from the Chinese sage, K'ung Fu-tse (c. 551–479 BC) – whom we in the West know from the Latinized version of his name as Confucius. The philosopher taught all the items covered in this dimension at various points in his (attributed) writings. He advocates both the ordering of relationships by status *and* stability, both thrift *and* reciprocation of favours and gifts, both a sense of shame *and* a respect for tradition. Bond noted that the items more emphasized on the dimension can be taken to imply a forward-looking, thrifty outlook supported by stable relationships and shame when offending them. The less emphasized items implied a more static preservation of traditional ways. Although all the values come from Confucius, the higher ones suggest a more dynamic approach and Bond therefore called this dimension *Confucian Dynamism*. Since this dimension was developed from Eastern values, it is not surprising that it is difficult for us of the West to appreciate fully the differences, and it must be underlined that they are those of relative emphasis within the Confucian framework.

Cultures high on this dimension appear to take a long-term view of the need for change. Hofsted (1991) subsequently generalized the naming of this dimension to long-term versus short-term orientation, since not all cultures which scored high (i.e. whose values were more dynamic) were influenced by Confucian philosophy. But remarkably all the most vigorous Asian economies were found to be high on this dimension. Thus what have become known as the 'Five Dragons of Asia', i.e. Japan, Taiwan, Hong Kong, South Korea and Singapore, appeared to have values which emphasize long-term returns and persistence towards slow results, rather than an emphasis on conforming to the demands of social status, face, unchanging tradition and quick results.

Activity 3

Please stop now and read the chapter on China from *Management Worldwide: The impact of societal culture on organizations around the globe* by Hickson and Pugh in your Supplemental Readings Book.

Since that description was written, the economic development of China has continued apace particularly in the special economic zones. Hong Kong has been reincorporated. The development of Shenzen in the south into what is intended to become the largest city in the world by the year 2015, demonstrates some of the largest economic growth rates in the world. Hofstede's survey puts China at the highest end on the Confucian Dynamism dimension, i.e. a persistently strong long-term orientation (Hofstede, 1991). This suggests that the Asian Dragons of Japan, Singapore, etc. might well be joined by the 'Giant Dragon' of China, although much more than cultural predisposition is required for economic achievement.

3.9 THE IMPACT OF CULTURAL DIFFERENCES

We have reviewed the work of Hofstede and his collaborators at some length because it is the most impressive of the systematic researches on this issue. It links world-wide attitude surveys with other descriptions of culture. But other attempts have been made to classify cultural differences in work (for example, Ronen, 1986; Trompenaars, 1993; Hickson and Pugh, 1995). They look at various dimensions, some that overlap with Hofstede's and some that tap other differences. So Hofstede's work is not presented as the final word, but only as a useful provisional framework for classifying national cultures and gaining some understanding of their differences.

There have been a number of criticisms of Hofstede's work, as is inevitable in all management research. We shall now examine four of them.

First, all Hofstede's original respondents came from one multinational corporation, IBM. We do not know clearly what effect this has had on the results. (Hofstede and his colleagues have since carried out other surveys not of IBM employees, but these are on a much much smaller scale than the original work.) Hofstede argues that the impact of the corporate culture of IBM would be to reduce national cultural differences, so his results are an underestimate of the differences which would be obtained if national organizations in different countries were studied. This may well be true; it is difficult to know. But it does mean that in the same cluster there will be work cultures that may vary much more in their values than do the staff in their IBM affiliates. Review Question 4 in Section 3.4 suggests that this might be the case for the UK and the USA.

The second criticism is that data represent values, that is, the attitudes of the IBM employees. Values certainly affect our behaviour, but they are not the only factor affecting it. Some of the factors we discussed in Section 2 will also have their impact, so that the resulting behaviour may be considerably different from what people report they think should happen when they fill in a questionnaire.

This is a major problem with much of the work in this field. There have been many more studies of what people say than of what they do. The typical approach is to do a systematic survey of attitudes, usually by questionnaire, and then illustrate it by anecdotes of what actually happens. That is why the Maurice study in Section 3.1 is important. It did not study the attitude variations of French and German managers, but examined the management structures, the salaries and the educational qualifications to demonstrate their differences. Similarly the study by Luthans and his colleagues comparing American and Russian managers, as discussed in Section 5.2 below, is important because it is based, not on questionnaire replies, but on actual regular systematic observation of the managers doing their jobs.

Third, Hofstede's analysis inevitably compresses and simplifies – after all that is what analysis is for. It characterizes national work cultures by taking the average for the respondents of each nation. This is a gross oversimplification since there will be a range of differences in people's attitudes in all cultures. It also leads to the danger of stereotyping.

In addition, as shown in Table 3 in Section 3.6, Hofstede develops a number of clusters of countries' work cultures (for example, Germanic, Nordic, Anglo) on the basis of the four dimensions. These dimensions are statistical abstractions. Each culture will have a unique configuration of positions on each dimension and these will interact to develop a unique work culture. So regarding Austria and Israel as Germanic, or the Netherlands and Norway as Nordic, or Ireland and Canada as Anglo, just because their scores are approximately the same, is not justified. The similarities are pretty rough, and the interactions of the particular differences will lead to very distinctive cultures.

This is the approach of those who argue that there is no escaping the need to study each culture in great depth and in its own terms. Classification into clusters is basically misleading.

The fourth criticism, taking the opposite approach to the third, is that Hofstede has overcomplicated his cultural maps. The dimensions have quite a considerable amount of overlap. Figure 3 in the Hofstede article in the Reader plots the scores on the power distance and individualism dimensions. You will see that cultures are very highly related: the countries with large power distance have a collectivist culture, while the countries with small power distance have an individualistic culture. There is only one country (Costa Rica) in the upper left-hand quadrant (small power distance and collectivist). There are five in the bottom right-hand quadrant (large power distance and individualist) but three of those are very near the edges, so hardly in the quadrant. With two exceptions (admittedly important ones, France and French-speaking Belgium) there is a very strong relationship between these two dimensions.

You have also seen that high- and low-context speech relates closely to the individualism–collectivism dimension. So does wealth, as measured by the gross domestic product per head of the population, and climate, when measured by the distance of a country's capital from the equator.

So, with a few exceptions, there is basically one dimension. At one end are the hot, poor, collectivist, large power distance cultures; at the other the cold, rich, individualist, small power distance cultures; and many cultures in between. This is the cultural analogue of underdevelopment, and you can see how it links in with the convergence thesis of Section 2. The fact that there is a correlation does not tell you which way the causal arrow goes. Are developed nations rich because they are individualistic in culture? Or are they individualistic because they are rich?

This is a complex issue to which the behaviour of the Asian Dragons is relevant. As we saw earlier, their economic success was achieved with a higher degree of collectivism than is characteristic of Western nations. With their current greater affluence, the question is whether their cultures will become more individualistic or not? There are some suggestions that Japan, for example, is becoming less collectivistically minded, as noted in Section 3.2. But these changes do not happen quickly and the next decade or so will tell.

3.10 CONCLUSION

The general import of Hofstede's work is that cultural differences have an overwhelming impact on how organizations function. Manufacturing consumer products or treating the sick in France, as distinct from Japan or the UK, calls for structures and processes that differ in many respects. Similarly, effective advertising of products and services must be different in the different clusters of cultures. (An advertising emphasis on the mystery and magic of a product, for instance, will not be appreciated in a high uncertainty-avoidance culture.) Since national cultures change so slowly, transfer of technology, knowledge and skills will always be reinterpreted by the receiving culture, and this will set strong limits on any tendencies to convergence that there might be.

4 WHAT MAKES AN EFFECTIVE CROSS-CULTURAL MANAGER?

4.1 THE NATURE OF CULTURE SHOCK

Our discussion so far in this unit has demonstrated that there is a range of differences in managerial operations in different cultures. The ever-increasing importance of international enterprise increases the need for managers who understand, and are effective in, cultures other than their own. This will be the case even if some convergence is taking place. Cultural flexibility is not easy to achieve because we are all subject – at least to some degree – to 'ethnocentrism'. This is the implicit assumption, often unawares, that our culture is the most important, our way of doing things is the natural way. So the French talk of '*Paris – capitale du monde*', the British of 'keeping Britain great' and the Chinese ideograph for China means 'the country at the centre of the Earth'. We all overestimate the importance of our country and our culture in the scheme of things. When we see something different in another culture, we are liable to view it as inferior to the comfortable practices and ways of thinking of our own past experience.

The development of this belief in our own culture is an important part of our ability to function effectively in it. But it is a feature of human nature that does provide problems when we come to operate in other cultures. It is the basis of 'culture shock'. This is the confusion that results from the feeling that you are 'out of your depth' in what is going on around you; you are struggling in a different culture because you cannot interpret the information that you are getting. What people do and what they say is puzzling and even offensive. All you know is that you are not coping as you do at home, and you resent this. It is an experience that almost all those who work in a different culture go through. Common results of not coping with the new culture are ineffectiveness in the job, alcoholism and divorce. Culture shock needs to be expected, understood and managed. Gullick (1990) describes the steps that people, including managers, are likely to go through when coming to stay and operate in a different culture for any length of time. These are:

1   arrival in new culture

2   spectator phase

3   increasing participation

4   first culture shock
    possible outcomes:
    (a) flight
    (b) going native
    (c) fight
    (d) adaptation

5   surface adjustment

6   mental isolation

7   second culture shock
    range of possible outcomes as in phase 4

8   adaptation.

Learning a new language is generally recognized as a considerable achievement, and learning to function effectively in a new culture has many similarities. But doing a good job in another land is often thought to flow directly from just technical, financial or managerial knowledge and experience. Someone who knows their job well, and is capable in their accustomed setting, is assumed to be equally capable elsewhere. It may therefore come as quite a shock for managers to discover that this is often not the case.

The first phase after arrival in a new country is the spectator phase where everything in the different culture is new and perplexing. The new arrival is often seen by the host country nationals as difficult or uncaring, since many mistakes are made through ignorance. Spectator expatriates are not able to see the implications of their mistakes from the locals' point of view. People who have to shop, cook, organize the household and communicate with servants, that is, engage with the new culture, cannot stay in this phase for long. But it is possible for senior managers to stay in it by operating entirely within their own organizations, which they continue to see in the same way as their organization back home. This is the 'colonial approach', and many UK subsidiaries abroad have tales of expatriate British managers who function only in English, and cause difficulties for their local colleagues. This style is dangerous because such managers may well make decisions without regard to cultural differences. They will then be less effective than they were at home, and will soon lose the confidence of their subordinates.

With the next phase of increasing participation, expatriates discover enough to avoid the more simple mistakes. They learn, for example, that there are different practices in the promptness of meetings and in the amount of general 'small talk' necessary before getting down to business. They have a greater sense of being able to communicate and being understood, and their own confidence increases. Major cultural differences are more readily recognized and attempts made to bridge them. Organizations can help in this stage by providing 'cultural gatekeepers' who are more knowledgeable and can help to overcome differences. These might be locals who can act as interpreters, or a specified manager who is more experienced in, and attuned to, the new culture. Gatekeepers would be called in to help smooth over any difficulties that arise.

This early confidence of the new manager soon wears thin, however, and is followed by the first culture shock, which takes the form of a large attack of discouragement. In this phase the overload of new information about what is going on around them is very oppressive. Managers feel that every contact is hard work, new ideas are always resisted, and the same work problem is always much harder to solve abroad than at home. They learn the hard way that, often, what sounds like 'yes' to a foreigner is in fact a polite way of saying 'no'. Problems of living conditions, lack of social life and homesickness crowd in. Expatriates tend to be driven back into themselves, and into the company of their fellow expatriates, and feel unable to rely on local help.

There are four possible ways of responding to culture shock:

1 Flight. Some managers leave the new culture shaking their heads at the impossibility of it all.

2 Going native. A few may fly in the other direction – into the host culture and an over-identification with it. This is the 'Lawrence of

Arabia syndrome'. They may even marry into the host culture, bring up their children to be monolingual, and make no attempt to bridge the cultures. They are often searching for a utopia in their adopted land and, if and when they fail to discover it, their second culture shock can be even greater than their first.

3 Fight. Managers attempt to run the operation as though it were in their home country by trying to force work procedures towards parent company ways of doing things. The resultant conflict is normally disastrous, if for no other reason than that the host country will be able to impose political and legal constraints in addition to cultural ones. There is rarely sufficient support to defend an expatriate who directly challenges host country attitudes and practices as the following example (Gullick, 1990) illustrates. Home country ways cannot be transplanted by force, and managers have to find other methods to proceed.

COME TO THE PARTY

Bob was a manager who worked in the Saudi Arabian office of a North American international construction company. He was proud that the company was 'American' and he always wanted to do things 'the American way'. When one of his colleagues was leaving to return home he wanted to organize a coffee party one afternoon to say farewell. He had great difficulty in getting his Arab subordinates to agree to come to the party although he pressed them hard. Eventually they complained to the higher management that Bob was trying to make them break the Ramadan fast. Bob was repatriated within a week for trying to impose home ways on the host culture.

4 Adaptation. Managers survive the first culture shock, which can last anything from a few days to several months and, by working hard to understand the new culture, can continue to function tolerably well and thus move on into the next phase.

This is the surface adjustment phase when the expatriate can operate fairly well in a limited range of activities and with a small group of friends. The newcomer will have discovered differences in polite conventions, notions of privacy, of giving and receiving gifts, and so on. Crucially, a manager will have begun to discover differences in attitudes to work and to feel that they are starting to understand them.

The mental isolation phase replaces that of surface adjustment. Managers want a deeper level of understanding, and more effective means of communicating, in order to improve operational efficiency. This is very difficult to bring about. They are thus led to continual personal analysis of the culture and of their performance in it in the hope of reaching home country levels of achievement. Expatriates are aware that they continue to make mistakes, even though these are now less obvious ones. As they come to realize that they know far less about the culture than they had supposed, the second culture shock sets in.

The second culture shock phase is at a more sophisticated level than the first. It may involve managers thinking very seriously about ethical issues. Managers are normally reasonably comfortable about what is immoral behaviour in their own cultures – they may not have felt it necessary even to think about such issues before. But in the new culture the operation of what is to them bribery (as in Nigeria), racial discrimination (as in Brazil) or child labour (as in China), may be different and more overtly challenging. Will they attempt to apply their own personal values and practices, which will cause immediate operational problems? Or will they adopt the behaviour of the host country, which may cause trouble with their top management who do not want accusations of malpractice made against their employees in the home country? Or will they make some uneasy compromise between the two? Managers will have to forge an ethical position on such issues, as much for themselves as for their organizations.

The second culture shock also leads to a degree of withdrawal and thought. The same four outcomes – flight, going native, fight, and adaptation – are possible.

The fourth outcome, the adaptation phase, occurs when a working knowledge of the culture has been attained. Realistic levels of communication and achievement are set. Expectations of what is possible are, in home country terms, lowered. An important development is the use of host country body language. In the Arab culture, for example, Western managers are regarded as 'shifty' until they learn to look directly into a colleague's eyes for the culturally appropriate longer amount of time than in the West. The ability to 'read' what is communicated by silence is a key skill. Relaxation is possible now for the expatriates, because they realize that some cross-cultural 'problems' exist which can be explained but not solved. It should be noted that this phase does not necessarily require expatriates to like the host culture. It does require that they be realistic about what can be achieved by a manager in a cross-cultural situation.

Activity 4 _____

Stop reading now and listen to the audio cassette programme *Expatriates*.

4.2 BEHAVIOURS OF EFFECTIVE CROSS-CULTURAL MANAGERS

Clearly, it is important for their own futures and for that of international enterprise, that successful cross-cultural managers learn how to adapt after both the first and second culture shock phases. What are the characteristics of managers who can successfully adapt to another culture and function effectively in it?

There are two immediate prerequisite conditions for an expatriate to be effective.

First, the individual must want to operate well in another culture and be excited by the challenge. Forced allocation to an overseas posting is a recipe for poor performance. And the same condition applies to the spouse. There is clear evidence that a spouse's adaptation is as critical to the success of the expatriate assignment as is the worker's. There are always difficult decisions and adjustments to be made about family issues, and the family as a whole must be interested in the benefits which this necessarily dislocating experience will bring to them. A spouse's job and career may have to change. The nature of housework and family caring may change considerably if the family accompanies the expatriate. And equally, family relationships will inevitably change if the family is separated and the manager can spend only limited periods at home when on leave.

Second, the individual must be prepared to make some attempt to learn the language for use at work, that is, beyond the purely touristic phrases. It is true that for many, if not most, multinational corporations the language of operation is English and senior managers will be able to interact in this language. But in non-English-speaking countries nationals do not use English when talking among themselves nor under conditions of stress. Expatriates who make no attempt to understand and contribute in the local language inevitably cut themselves off from anything more than the surface adjustment phase. Except in quasi-colonial situations, they are unlikely to survive the second culture shock to reach the adaptation phase.

Ratiu (1983) conducted a study among 250 younger international managers of 35 different nationalities who were attending post-graduate programmes at two European business schools: INSEAD at Fontainebleau in France and the London Business School in the UK. The average age of those studied was 27 years, and most had at least three years' overseas experience. All spoke at least two languages and all wished to continue international careers. They thus all had the two prerequisites of commitment to international experience and active development of fluency in another language. They had also had opportunities to go through the phases of adjustment described above.

Even among this internationally experienced group, interesting differences were found. In an anonymous survey, 10 per cent of each group were rated 'most international'. What further characterizes such successful international managers? They were described by their fellows as 'flexible', 'open-minded', 'has many friends of different nationalities' and 'speaks with others in their own language'. Not all the descriptions were complimentary though: terms like 'chameleon-like' and 'unplaceable' were also used. When the researcher discussed with the managers which key learning experiences were associated with becoming more internationally minded, some very interesting differences arose between the 'most international' and the rest, whom we will refer to as the 'other international' managers. The differences are summarized in Table 4 and discussed below.

In Table 4, Ratiu has polarized two extreme attitudes with regard to attempts to cope in another culture. The 'most international' managers are seen to be very flexible and subjective in their thinking. They treat each person and each occurrence on their own merits trying intuitively to feel what approach is required. They are always ready to try something else if the current approach fails. Everybody inevitably uses stereotypes, but the 'most international' do so only tentatively at the beginning of an experience, and privately. They avoid giving blanket characterizations and 'public stereotyping'. They try to be descriptive of the actual situation and avoid being too analytical. (The examples below illustrate the difference in approach between a 'most international' and an 'other international' manager.) They therefore, rather paradoxically, do not characterize themselves as 'most international' – they don't believe in such types – but merely talk about the need to describe new experiences and to think what can be done about them. This forward orientation contrasts with the 'other international' managers who often take an

Table 4 Comparison of approaches of managers	
'Most international'	**'Other international'**
Goal is to be able to adapt to individual people	Goal is to be able to adapt to the culture
Asks questions about what is happening	Asks questions about why this is happening
Looks for descriptions, meaning	Looks for explanations, reasons
Feelings and impressions are relevant information	Only facts are relevant information
Differentiates cultures qualitatively without comparing them	Compares and evaluates cultures quantitatively
Uses impressions to modify and clarify private stereotypes	Uses impressions to confirm theories and public stereotypes

(Source: adapted from Ratiu, 1983, p. 146)

analytical view in trying to explain the new situations. It is a view which can often come from a backward orientation.

UNDERSTANDING OTHER CULTURES

For the 'most international' managers in the Ratiu study things are assumed to be not what they seem. Experiences are continually being labelled and relabelled since the labelling is assumed to be unreliable and must be constantly checked against the new information of unfolding events. Speaking of Britain one such manager said:

> 'I've been finding out more and more ... Arabs absolutely abound in this country, much more than I thought possible. And I mean a Bristol man, is not a Sheffield man, is not a Darlington man, is not a ... you know ... it's incredible.'

> *(Ratiu, 1983, p. 144)*

The 'other international' managers have a more analytical approach. Their emphasis is less on information collection and more on early explanation and rapid conclusions. One of them said:

> 'Why was it that every time there was a technical hitch on site, a breakdown of some kind, I was quite unable to get it across to the operators, both Yemenis, that there was a perfectly straightforward technical reason? For them it was always God's will: "Nothing can be done about it because God willed it so." At first, I just couldn't understand it. But having lived out in the desert for centuries as these people have, subject to the kind of harsh climate they are used to, and with little or no control over its effects, you would expect them to adopt this kind of attitude. To us it seems very passive, but it's really quite understandable. Later I moved to Saudi Arabia. And, sure enough, people there behaved in exactly the same way. I wonder if this sort of passivity isn't typical of the Arabs generally.'

> *(p. 145)*

Compared with the 'most international' manager, the approach here is very ambitious, in fact looking for a theory to explain the events. This leads to the 'public stereotyping' displayed.

An interesting characteristic of the 'most international' managers is the ease and readiness with which they can recall and discuss the stress symptoms they experienced as part of the culture shock. They regard culture shock as a positive learning experience. The 'other international' managers, on the other hand, refer to it only obliquely and with discomfort as an example of failure. The 'most internationals' deal with the stress involved by having 'stability zones' to which they can temporarily withdraw. Examples of stability zones include personal pastimes such as playing chess, writing up a diary, meditation, and religious practice. This approach allows a rhythm of high participation alternating with short withdrawal periods which enables the managers to carry on working effectively in the new environment. In contrast the 'other international' managers seek to cope by restricting their general level of involvement in the new culture and spending much more time with fellow expatriates.

The distinctions between the 'most international' managers and the others has been presented in a very polarized way. Many people are likely to be in-between in their attitudes: aiming for maximum flexibility and multicultural effectiveness but often resorting to the more rigid approach. However, the polarization does indicate the behaviours to aim for in order to achieve greater cross-cultural effectiveness.

4.3 DOES TRAINING HELP TO PRODUCE EFFECTIVE CROSS-CULTURAL MANAGERS?

Probably yes. But it has got to be good training. There is evidence to show that bad training programmes can actually reduce the effectiveness of the participants when they move to their new postings. This is probably because the training is too superficial and succeeds only in giving the managers a false sense of confidence in their ability to cope effectively with cultural differences. They are therefore less open to what they encounter, believing that they know it already.

There are two basic elements to the training required – the development of general intercultural skills and knowledge of the specific cultural environment. Hawthorne *et al.* (1990) describe the approach of one company that takes cross-cultural awareness training seriously.

THE HONG KONG AND SHANGHAI BANK INTERNATIONAL TRAINING PROGRAMME

Graduate trainees in the international stream of the Hong Kong and Shanghai Bank have opted to be available for posting to any of the Bank's operations world wide. They undertake a six-month executive development programme which draws participants from all over the world. As many as ten nationalities will be working together on a programme which develops technical and managerial skills and gives a range of opportunities to develop cultural sensitivity and build cultural synergy.

There are four stages in the programme. The first is an initial orientation and team-building seminar to develop cultural awareness. The second stage is a ten-day outdoor personal development course conducted in multicultural teams. It provides participants with experience of such overt cultural differences as cleanliness, dress, eating habits and attitudes towards privacy. It also requires them to come to terms with implicit cultural differences in trust, participation and interpersonal relations, thus developing the skills needed to cope effectively in any new culture.

The third stage is a week's interpersonal skills course, and in the fourth stage participants have to undertake an international assignment working in a culture different from their own. Attachments after the programme may not be to the initial posting because the aim is to develop general cultural sensitivity, not simply specific knowledge of another culture.

When a manager has gained insight and skills for operating in any new culture, it is then necessary to obtain good knowledge about the specific context. Intellectual knowledge of, for example, business practices, the nature of markets, and the level of technical knowledge of staff, has to be put in the context of the characteristic attitudes of the particular culture to authority, change, achievement, time, and so on. There is clearly a great deal to be learnt.

Brislin *et al.* (1986) list eight knowledge areas which returning expatriates regularly identify as causing difficulties and misunderstandings. These are in addition to the usual subjective stresses that working in a new environment causes, such as anxiety about the unfamiliar, feelings of lack of belonging, and confrontation with one's own prejudices. The knowledge areas are:

1 work (e.g. the balance between task effort and social interaction)

2 time and space (e.g. time keeping for meetings, appropriate distance from colleagues when talking)

3 language (e.g. higher- or lower-context speech)

4 roles (e.g. the authoritarian content in the manager's role)

5 group demands versus an individual's needs

6 rituals and superstitions (which are likely to be different and challenging, since few of us recognize our own culture's rituals but instead tend to think we don't have any!)

7 class and status (e.g. the marks of high and low status)

8 values (e.g. concerning what is desirable in politics, economics, the environment).

Building on the work of Fiedler *et al.* (1971) on the 'Cultural Assimilator', Brislin and his colleagues advocate a training method to encourage early cross-cultural preparation by working through a series of short case studies. These critical incidents allow managers to obtain some of the appropriate knowledge, as listed above, that will be required when working in a new culture. The large number of cases has been developed to be assimilated through continued use in real situations, rather than as descriptive material to be learnt by heart. Review Question 5 gives an example of one of the case incidents. Test your current level of awareness of the differences between French and Japanese business cultures by answering the question.

Review Questions 5

Read the following case incident and answer the question.

Engineering a decision

Mr Legrand is a French engineer who works for a Japanese company in France. One day the general manager, Mr Tanaka, called him into his office to discuss a new project in the Middle East. He told Mr Legrand that the company is very pleased with his dedicated work and would like him to act as chief engineer for the project. It would mean two to three years away from home, but his family would be able to accompany him and there would be considerable financial benefits to the position – and, of course, he would be performing a valuable service to the company. Mr Legrand thanked Mr Tanaka for the confidence he has in him but said he would have to discuss it with his wife before deciding. Two days later he returns and tells Mr Tanaka that both he and his wife do not like the thought of leaving France and so he does not want to accept the position. Mr Tanaka says nothing but is somewhat dumbfounded by his decision.

Why is Mr Tanaka so bewildered by Mr Legrand's decision? CHOOSE ONE OPTION.

1 He believes it is foolish for Mr Legrand to refuse all the financial benefits that go with the position.

2 He cannot accept that Mr Legrand should take any notice of his wife's opinion in the matter.

3 He believes that Mr Legrand is possibly trying to bluff him into offering greater incentives to accept the offer.

4 He feels it is not appropriate for Mr Legrand to place his personal inclinations above those of his role as an employee of the company.

(Brislin et al., 1986, pp. 158–9)

Equipped with some sensitivity to cultural differences and some knowledge of the host culture, a manager will be in a better position to cope effectively with the expatriate assignment. When it is over, the manager will often be returning home – only to discover that another set of cultural adjustments is required!

4.4 CONCLUSION

We list below ten steps to becoming a successful international manager.

1 You must want to become an international manager and find the challenge exciting.

2 Develop your global knowledge and thinking. Work to understand your own industry, including your organization's competitors, on a world-wide scale. Read appropriate international trade journals to keep up with global developments.

3 Do all you can to ensure that your family also understand and accept the challenge of multicultural living.

4 Make an effort to learn the appropriate foreign language for a work context, not just a touristic one.

5 Obtain good preparatory training which not only covers information about the new country, but focuses on cross-cultural interpersonal skills and managerial functioning.

6 Understand the adjustment process, including the inevitable culture shock, and manage your way through it.

7 Watch and listen very carefully, being continually prepared to update your views of particular individuals and situations.

8 Set yourself realistic objectives on the job, taking account of the new culture as well as of parent company standards.

9 Work to forge your own ethical position and understand its justification.

10 Develop and regularly use stability zones to help in your adjustment. Create opportunities for 'letting go' which allow you to return to the host culture with high energy.

Finally, be prepared for culture shock on returning to your own country and your own organization. This too must be understood and managed. The more successful you have been in adjusting to another culture, the greater this culture shock will be.

5 CULTURAL CHANGE

We have now reviewed, even if only in an introductory way, the impact of culture on management. The Marketing unit looks at culture in more depth as it impinges upon marketing. Whole books can be, and have been, written on this issue. In this section, we bring together the arguments of Sections 2 and 3, to see if we can understand the processes of cultural change which are taking place.

5.1 THE PROCESSES OF CULTURAL CHANGE

In spite of the evidence in Section 2 of a global convergence in management operations, there are still considerable cultural differences, as Sections 3 and 4 have illustrated. So, even though the institutional contexts and management structures of two organizations might be the same, if they are in different countries the people in them will behave differently. This is because the people are functioning in their different cultures into which they have been socialized from birth.

A key dimension of organizational structure was shown to be centralization in the Aston studies described in Section 2.4. Similarly, the Hofstede study found that a key dimension of cultural difference in work attitudes is power distance. Since both these dimensions are concerned with aspects of hierarchy, they might be expected to map on to each other: centralization and high power distance would go together, and decentralization and low power distance. Let us examine this possible relationship more closely.

The Aston studies demonstrated that the degree of centralization of the formal decision-making structure is highly influenced by the context in which the organization has to operate. Government- or family-owned organizations will be more centralized than corporately-owned ones. Dependent firms, which are closely tied in with their suppliers or customers, will be more centralized than less dependent ones. Certain technologies will require greater centralization; others greater decentralization. This has been shown to be true in a large range of cultures. So the first point to note is that all cultures can support a range of both more centralized and more decentralized decision-making structures.

The Hofstede study showed that for each national culture there is a distinctive position on the power distance dimension. So, to take two countries far apart in Figure 3 of the Hofstede Reader article, many members of the US culture (but by no means all) would hold the low power distance value of participation, whilst many members (but not all) of the Venezuelan culture would hold the high power distance value of deference.

There are both more centralized and less centralized firms in both countries. We should expect that centralized firms in Venezuela would run smoothly since the managers would be happy to refer decisions to ever-higher authority. Decentralized firms would have more difficulty. The managers would find it more difficult to take responsibility for decisions and, by pushing them upwards to their bosses, would in practice be making the firm more centralized. In the USA it would be the other way round. Centralized organizations would continually be subject to the pressures of lower levels wanting to take decisions, or at least to participate in them, which would in practice be making the firm more decentralized. Whether particular firms with particular structures are successful would depend on the demands of the technology and the environment. It is the convergers' case that these factors are continually becoming more global in their effects and pushing developments towards convergence. The example below is described in Trompenaars (1993).

THE PROBLEM OF THE DEPUTY MANAGER

The American manager of a plant processing and packaging PVC in the USA had a Venezuelan deputy. The process required a high standard of quality control. The product had to be mixed in exactly the correct proportions or it was dangerous. Irregularity in mixing and blending had to be reported immediately it occurred and the line concerned closed down at once; otherwise unsaleable product would accumulate. A decision to shut down was an expert one requiring detailed technical knowledge. Even a delay of minutes was extremely costly. It was better on the whole to shut down prematurely than to shut down too late.

The Venezuelan deputy knew very well when the product was satisfactory and when it was not. When his manager was away from the plant and he was in charge, he brought any line whose quality was failing to an immediate halt. His judgement was both fast and accurate. When the manager was there, however, he would look for him, report what was happening and get a decision. In the time it took to do this, considerable product was wasted. However many times the deputy was told to act on his own, that his judgement was respected and that his decision would be upheld, he always reverted to his original practice.

The problem was a clash between two cultural attitudes. In a low power distance approach, it is not very important who takes the decision provided it is the correct one. Whether it is the boss or the deputy is determined by the needs of the technology and the task. In a high power distance culture, a boss is like a father and you do not usurp his authority when he is present.

The interesting question is what is going to happen in the long-term. Can the US PVC firm go on operating less efficiently than it might in order to accommodate the high power distance attitudes of the Venezuelan deputy manager? As the firm is interested in efficiency, probably not – he will either have to change or go. But what about such a PVC plant in Venezuela? Can it survive if the high power distance attitudes there make it less efficient? In the short-term, yes, for there will no doubt be other efficiencies, such as lower labour costs. But in the longer-term, the convergence thesis would argue that all possible methods of operating the costly high-tech plant to maximum efficiency will push for a more decentralized approach in the deputy's job even there. Perhaps, in the first instance, this could be achieved by appointing a Venezuelan with lower power distance attitudes. It is important to remember that there will be many such managers. Hofstede's characterization of Venezuela is a blanket one for the whole country and cannot apply equally to 20 million people. Maybe the manager chosen will have trained in a US plant. He will ruffle feathers at first, of course, and people will think that what he is doing is 'pushy'. But if he perseveres and succeeds, the culture will change, even though slowly, and will converge on the need to run the technology efficiently.

Conversely, there will be examples in other countries of where a low power distance attitude will have to change to a higher one in order to operate efficiently. It is interesting that cultural change in this direction appears to be easier for managers to develop. These slow changes of attitudes and behaviour when cultures come into contact with other cultures are characteristic of the way cultural development takes place.

These small behavioural changes are always difficult to discover and interpret. The next section describes a direct study of the actual behaviour of US and Russian managers.

5.2 WHAT DO MANAGERS IN THE USA AND RUSSIA ACTUALLY DO?

Luthans and his colleagues have studied what managers in the USA actually do. They observed the managers in a large number of diverse organizations and classified their activities into a predesigned set of behavioural categories. In 1990 (well into *perestroika*, but before the break-up of the Soviet Union) they collaborated with Russian colleagues to conduct precisely the same study on a sample of managers in a textile mill generally recognized to be one of the largest and most efficient in Russia (Luthans *et al.*, 1993).

The analytical scheme for describing the managers' behaviour had 63 behavioural descriptions, for example, hires staff, decides what to do, processes mail, coaches subordinates. These were organized into 13 sub-categories, for example, planning, managing conflict, interacting with outsiders. (In both the USA and Russia a proposed category of 'disciplining/punishing' personnel had to be dropped because the managers did not want this activity to be observed by outside researchers.) The data were collected by requiring trained observers to fill in a checklist of what behaviour was taking place on 80 occasions over two weeks in a predetermined, random, 10-minute period in each working hour.

Four overall analytical categories were set up, based on the 13 sub-categories:

1 traditional management activities, including planning, decision making, monitoring, controlling performance

2 communication activities, including exchanging routine information, processing paperwork

3 human resource management activities, including motivating, staffing, managing conflict

4 networking activities, including socializing, politicking, interacting with outsiders.

The frequencies of each activity in both the US and Russian management samples are given in Table 5.

Table 5 Relative frequencies of managerial activities

Managerial activities	Russian sample 66 participants (%)	US sample 248 participants (%)
Traditional management	43	32
Communication	34	29
Human resource management	15	20
Networking	9	19

There were further interesting findings.

- More successful managers (defined as the relationship between age and job grade – more successful managers were younger ones in higher grades) were likely to spend more time on networking activities than less successful ones.

- More effective managers (defined on the basis of ratings by their subordinates) were more likely to emphasize communication activities than less effective ones.

- Both the above findings were true of both the Russian and the US samples.

Review Question 6

Based on the results of the Luthans *et al.* study, how similar would you regard the jobs that the US and Russian managers were doing? List some facts which suggest they are similar. List some factors which would lead you to think that the jobs are very different.

5.3 WHAT IS A CONSIDERATE SUPERVISOR?

Although there are clear similarities across cultures in what managers do, there will also be differences – often within those similarities! Smith *et al.* (1989) studied supervisory behaviour in electronics assembly plants in the USA, Hong Kong, Japan and the UK. In all the plants studied, supervisors who were 'considerate' towards the members of their work teams were evaluated positively. So consideration appears to be a global value. But when workers were asked to indicate which of a number of behaviours their supervisors should exhibit to be regarded as considerate, it was found that supervisors have to do rather different things to earn approval in the different countries.

For example, one question asked what a supervisor should do if a member of the team is experiencing personal difficulties. In two of the countries workers said that to discuss the problem with other members of the team in the worker's absence would be a considerate thing to do. But in the two other countries, on the contrary, any public discussion was regarded as a very inconsiderate thing to do. Clearly, although consideration is a general virtue, the behaviours that are entailed may be very different. This is a general point. It is often difficult to get behind the words used to the actual behaviour. And even here it must be pointed out that the Smith *et al.* study was based on people's verbal responses, not actual behaviour.

Review Question 7 _____

In which two cultures in the Smith *et al.* study in factories in the USA, Hong Kong, Japan and the UK do you think a considerate supervisor was regarded as:

(a) one who discussed the worker's personal problems with the remaining members of the group

(b) one who did not discuss the worker's personal problems with the remaining members of the group?

List the reasons for your choice.

5.4 CONVERGENCE REVIEWED

We have considered some of the arguments and evidence on the convergence issue. So we may now ask how far convergence is taking place at the level of management functioning.

The strength of the convergers' case rests upon the fact that tasks need to be done effectively. This influences the macro aspects of technology and thus must affect organizational behaviour world wide. The divergers' case rests on cultural differences in thinking, attitudes and values which will always act to interpret the same technological and system changes differently in different cultures. It is certainly true that the world is getting smaller, with easier and cheaper communications, travel and trade, and this supports the convergers. But it is also true that the gaps between the 'have' and the 'have-not' nations are not narrowing, which acts against the developing countries' moving towards Western-style efficiency.

One view might be that the convergers and the culturalists are both right. While the culture sets limits to what changes will be acceptable, it is the convergence pressures for efficiency that inaugurate those changes. Under some conditions (for example, with rapidly developing technology) the pressures for convergence may gather enough momentum to win completely, but under other conditions (for example, intermediate levels of economic activity) quite significant differences may remain to generate different but equally viable organizational processes and behaviour. The pressures towards convergence are quite considerable. Even US organizations (surely operating in a culture that can be considered economically viable) are being pressed to accept aspects of Japanese organizational culture which have been held to be more efficient. But the ability of many cultures to accept outside technology, knowledge and skills, and re-interpret them to fit with only very slow changes, will set strong limits on any convergent tendencies that there might be.

There is at present no unequivocal answer to the convergence/culture specific issue. Both the changes and the debate continue.

CONCLUSION TO THE UNIT

This unit has only touched on the topic of culture. Anthropologists and sociologists the world over make a life's work of studying the topic in detail. What we have tried to do here is to show you the kinds of things that make up culture (attitudes towards authority, others, self and nature) and to give you a way to think about how cultures might vary on four dimensions: power distance, uncertainty avoidance, masculinity and individualism.

But we have also argued that the world's cultures (at least in the aspects relevant to organizations) are converging. Technology, be it the mechanical technology necessary to produce goods or information technology, requires similar procedures to be employed effectively no matter where you are. Organizational structure is, to a great extent, influenced by organizational size and scope no matter where the home organization is located.

We have also tried to show you how cultural variation impinges on the tasks of international managers, and how expatriates experience culture shock in their encounters with new cultures. We showed you why training for expatriate managers is crucial, and developed a description of effective international managers.

Finally, we will leave you with the idea that an understanding of both the similarities and differences between cultures underlies almost all work across borders. Too strong an emphasis on cultural differences overemphasizes the importance of culture in our managerial action. Too strong an emphasis on similarity leads to culturally inappropriate behaviour. The only remedy for this is clear understanding of not only the cultures with which we deal, but our own culture as well.

'OK, does anyone find THIS one offensive?'

REFERENCES

ADLER, N.J. (1991) *International Dimensions of Organizational Behaviour* (2nd ed.), Boston, Mass., PWS-Kent Publishing.
A good introduction to the personal aspects of managing in multicultural situations.

BALLON, R.J. (1983) 'Non-western work organization', *Asia Pacific Journal of Management*, Vol. 1, pp. 1–14.

BANAI, M. (1997) 'Children of the system: management in Russia', in Clark, T. (ed.) *Advancement in Organizational Behaviour: Essays in honour of Derek S. Pugh*, Aldershot, Ashgate.

BRISLIN, R.W., CUSHNER, K., CHERRIE, C. and YONG, M. (1986) *Intercultural Interactions: a practical guide*, London, Sage.
A useful series of short case incidents to encourage learning about different cultures.

DORE, R. (1973) *British Factory – Japanese Factory*, London, Allen and Unwin.

DUBIN, R. (1970) 'Management in Britain: observations of a visiting professor', *Journal of Management Studies*, Vol. 7, pp. 183–98.

EBSTER - GROSZ, D. and PUGH, D.S. (1996) *Anglo-German Business Collaboration: Pitfalls and Potentials*, Basingstoke, Macmillan.

FIEDLER, F.E., MITCHELL, T. and TRIANDIS, H. (1971) 'The cultural assimilator: an approach to cross-cultural training', *Journal of Applied Psychology*, Vol. 55, pp. 95–102.

GALBRAITH, J.K. (1978) *The New Industrial State* (revised ed.), Harmondsworth, Penguin.

GULLICK, C.J.M.R. (1990) 'Expatriate British managers and culture shock', in *Studies in Third World Societies*, No. 42, Williamsburg, Virginia, Department of Social Anthropology, College of William and Mary, pp. 173–206.

GUY, V. and MATTOCK, J. (1993) *The New International Manager*, London, Kogan Page.

HALL, E.T. (1976) *Beyond Culture*, New York, Doubleday.
A classic book from one of the most insightful writers on cultural differences in management.

HAWTHORNE, P., TANG, S. and KIRKBRIDE, P. (1990) 'Creating the culturally sensitive Hong Kong bank manager', *EFMD Journal*, No. 4, pp. 14–17.

HICKSON, D.J. and PUGH, D.S. (1995) *Management Worldwide: The impact of societal culture on organizations around the globe*, London, Penguin.
An analysis of the impact of culture on management in 18 different countries.

HOFSTEDE, G. (1980) *Culture's Consequences*, London, Sage.

HOFSTEDE, G. (1991) *Cultures and Organizations*, Maidenhead, McGraw-Hill.
The author links his national cultural dimensions with organizational culture.

HOFSTEDE, G. and BOND, M.H. (1988) 'The Confucius connection: from cultural roots to economic growth', *Organizational Dynamics*, Vol. 16, pp. 4–21.

KERR, C., DUNLOP, J.T., HARBISON, F.H. and MYERS, C.A. (1960) *Industrialism and Industrial Man*, Harvard, Harvard University Press.

LUTHANS, F., WELSH, D.H.B. and ROSENKRANTZ, S.A. (1993) 'What do Russian managers really do? An observational study with comparisons to US managers', *Journal of International Business Studies*, Vol. 24, pp. 741–61.

MAURICE, M. (1979) 'For a study of the societal effect: universality and specificity in organization research', in Lammers, C.J. and Hickson, D.J. (eds) *Organizations Alike and Unlike*, London, Routledge.

MUNA, F. (1980) *The Arab Executive*, London, St Martin's Press.

OUCHI, W. (1981) *Theory Z: how American business can meet the Japanese challenge*, Reading, Mass., Addison-Wesley.

PUGH, D.S. (ed.) (1997) *Organization Theory: selected readings* (4th ed.), London, Penguin.

PUGH, D.S. (ed.) (1998) *The Aston Programme, Vols. I, II and III*, Classic research in management series, Aldershot, Ashgate – Dartmouth.

RATIU, I. (1983) 'Thinking internationally: a comparison of how international executives learn', *International Studies of Management and Organization*, Vol. 13, pp. 139–50.

RONEN, S. (1986) *Comparative and International Management*, New York, Wiley.
A comprehensive textbook of the field including a review of a number of classifications of culture.

SCHOLZ, C. (1996) 'Human resource management in Germany', in Clark, T. (ed.) *European Human Resource Management*, Oxford, Blackwell.

SEMIN, G.R. and RUBINI, M. (1990) 'Unfolding the concept of person by verbal abuse', *European Journal of Social Psychology, Vol. 20, pp. 463–74.*

SMITH, P.B. and BOND, M.H. (1993) *Social Psychology Across Cultures*, Hemel Hempstead, Harvester Wheatsheaf.
A thoughtful review of the problems of cultural differences, concentrating on the social psychological aspects.

SMITH, P.B., MISUMI, J., TAYEB, M., PETERSON, M.F. and BOND, M.H. (1989) 'On the generality of leadership styles across cultures', *Journal of Occupational Psychology*, Vol. 62, pp. 97–100.

STEELE, F. (1977) 'Is the culture hostile to organization development?: the UK example', in Mervis, P.H. and Berg, D.N. (eds), *Failures in Organization Development and Change*, New York, Wiley.

TANNENBAUM, A.S. (1986) 'Controversies about control and democracy in Organizations', in Stern, R.N. and McCarthy, S. (eds), *The International Yearbook of Organizational Democracy, Vol. III*, Chichester, Wiley.

TAYLOR, F.W. (1912) 'Testimony to the House of Representative's Committee on Scientific Management', reprinted in PUGH (1997) (op. cit.).

TROMPENAARS, F. (1993) *Riding the Waves of Culture*, London, Nicholas Brealey.
Another attempt to classify cultures using very many business examples.

USUNIER, J.C. (1996) *Marketing Across Cultures* (2nd ed.), Hemel Hempstead, Prentice Hall, Europe.

COMMENTS ON REVIEW QUESTIONS

Review Question 1

French firms are higher on the power distance dimension than German ones. In a French organization an élite group comes in higher up the organization. The members of this élite are better qualified and better paid; they take more decisions and set more procedures from above. Those below cannot aspire to join the élite. In German firms there is not this barrier, and promotion is possible in smaller steps further up the organization. More decisions are delegated, and junior managers are better qualified and better paid.

Review Question 2

Japanese culture is extremely high on uncertainty avoidance. Examples of characteristics include: hard work, lifelong career structure, respect and power given to age, great identification with country and organization, intolerance of deviancy, and importance of consensus decision making.

Review Question 3

The Arab executive culture is low on individualism and higher on collectivism. Examples of characteristics include: lack of separation of business affairs from social life, strong kinship structure and 'nepotism', paramount importance of loyalty and trust among own group.

Review Question 4

(a) US management culture is higher on masculinity. There is a greater stress on achievement, as measured by objective criteria, and innovations to bring better achievements are more likely. In the UK the feminine values of 'fitting in' and 'not rocking the boat' are rated more highly, as is a greater willingness to tolerate inadequate subordinates. Social acceptability is given greater weight in relation to task capability than in the USA.

This answer is based on the work of Dubin and Steele as described in this section. As a matter of fact, Hofstede's own research places the UK and the USA at about the same score on this dimension. As we shall see below, they are placed in the same cluster of cultures. A possible reason for this difference in results is that all the respondents in the Hofstede survey were IBM employees whose values are taken to represent their national cultures. But it could be that, as a US-founded multinational with a strong corporate culture, IBM recruited more 'American'-oriented people in Britain; in other words, they were a biased sample in regard to British cultural work values.

(b) Cultures develop, and certainly the considerable reduction of workforces may well have pushed the British work culture to be more concerned with efficiency and profitability than previously. A more 'masculine' work culture would then have developed. While

we know of no systematic research on this topic, many British managers with experience of the last 20 years seem to agree that a certain amount of cultural change has taken place.

Review Question 5

These are the comments of Brislin et al. *on the options:*

1 *There is little evidence of this in the story. While the financial benefits are relevant, to Mr Tanaka they are probably a minor consideration in the situation. Please choose another response.*

2 *It is quite probable that, coming from a male-dominant Japanese society, he does think it odd that Mr Legrand should mention his wife's opinion. However, the decision not to go to the Middle East also appears to be Mr Legrand's personal inclination, so this does not fully account for Mr Tanaka's bewilderment. There is another explanation. Please choose again.*

3 *It is unlikely that Mr Tanaka would consider this. There are factors far removed from personal gain dominating his concern. Please choose again.*

4 *This is the most likely explanation. In Japan, and many other collectivist societies, a person is defined much more as a collection of roles (parent, employee, servant, official) than by his or her individual identity. As such, fulfilling each of these roles to the best of one's ability is regarded as more important than one's personal inclinations. Thus Mr Tanaka would see that Mr Legrand's responsibility as a company employee would be to accept the position whether or not he is happy about the idea. Mr Legrand's refusal is thus bewildering and makes him think that his belief in Mr Legrand's dedication has been completely misplaced. Mr Legrand, however, comes from a culture where individual freedoms are highly valued and so exercises his right to refuse the option with little compunction. The cultural conflict thus resides in different strengths of values applied to the roles occupied by a person in the culture.*

(p.177)

(Brislin et al., 1986 p. 177)

Review Question 6

Table 5 shows some small, but interesting, differences in the analytical categories. The Russian managers spent more time on traditional management activities and less on networking than the US managers in the sample. This may be due to differences in the culture or to the effects of the important changes with which Russian managers have to cope. But clearly, in general, the tasks of both sets of managers when analysed under these general headings cover the same range and would seem to be very comparable. The fact that successful and effective managers in both countries were differentiated from their colleagues in the same way again emphasizes the comparability of the management processes.

But, of course, such an analysis goes only so far. It does not look at the actual content of the various categories, for example, which control decisions had to be made, how the staff were motivated, who was politicking with whom, about what. At this level of analysis, the jobs are likely to show great differences. Most Russians have lived and worked in the Communist system, where bureaucracies were supreme. They worked to a government plan, decisions were always taken 'higher up' and everyone did as they were told, or bent their energies to fiddle the system. So perhaps it is not surprising that Luthans' group also showed that the introduction of greater participation in decision-making led to a decrease in performance.

Banai (1997) in a study of how Russian managers are trying to cope with the introduction of Western free-market economics, concludes that it will take a generation – the time needed for the present managers to retire, and younger ones who were not in the old system to succeed them – for the new system to work in anything like the way it does in the West. For this reason Western firms are finding that, in the running of their Russian subsidiaries, they have to make more use of expatriate managers and less of indigenous Russians than they expected.

Review Question 7

(a) In Hong Kong and Japan a considerate supervisor would discuss a worker's personal problems with other members of the group. These cultures are collectivist with high-context speech. As the emphasis is on 'we', the group would want to help. They have a moral commitment to the organization and an emotional dependence on its members. Since they have high-context speech, the group members would want to know about the problems so that they would allude to them only by saying what is appropriate, thus avoiding bringing any challenge or shame on the worker.

(b) In the USA and the UK a considerate supervisor would not discuss a worker's personal problems with other members of the group. These cultures are individualist with low-context speech. Identity is based on the individual, and there is only limited specific job commitment to the work organization. The work group, as a group, would not regard it as proper to be concerned with personal non-work problems. Since the speech is low context, a worker who wants personal help can ask another individual directly. That person, even if they are the supervisor, should not disclose to others what is said about a non-work issue.

ACKNOWLEDGEMENTS

Grateful acknowledgement is made to the following sources for permission to reproduce material in this unit:

Illustrations

Front cover: NASA; *Figure 1:* Hickson, D.J. and Pugh, D.S. (1995) *Management Worldwide: The impact of societal culture on organizations around the globe*, Penguin Books Ltd, copyright © D.J. Hickson and D.S. Pugh, 1995; *Figure 2:* adapted from Trompenaars, F. (1993) *Riding the Waves of Culture*, Nicholas Brealey Publishers Ltd.

Tables

Table 2: adapted from Hall, E.T. (1976) *Beyond Culture*, Doubleday & Co. Inc.; *Table 3:* adapted from Hofstede, G. (1980) *Culture's Consequences*, Sage Publications Ltd.